WHAT YOU NEED TO KNOW ABOUT

SPIRITUAL GROWTH

IN 12 LESSONS

MAX ANDERS

THOMAS NELSON PUBLISHERS
Nashville

Library of Congress Cataloging-in-Publication Data

Anders, Max E., 1947–
   Spiritual growth / by Max Anders.
      p.   cm. — (What you need to know about)
   Includes bibliographical references.
   ISBN 0-8407-1936-1 (pbk.)
   1. Spiritual life—Christianity.   2. Spiritual formation.
   I. Title. II. Series.
BV4501.2.A4555   1997   97-8578
248—dc21   CIP

Printed in the United States of America

1 2 3 4 5 6 7 8—02 01 00 99 98 97

Contents

Introduction to the
What You Need to Know Series

You hold in your hands a tool with enormous potential—the ability to help ground you, and a whole new generation of other Christians, in the basics of the Christian faith.

I believe the times call for just this tool. We face a serious crisis in the church today . . . namely, a generation of Christians who know the truth but who do not live it. An even greater challenge is coming straight at us, however: a coming generation of Christians who may not even know the truth!

Many Christian leaders agree that today's evangelical church urgently needs a tool flexible enough to be used by a wide variety of churches to ground current and future generations of Christians in the basics of Scripture and historic Christianity.

This guide, and the whole series from which it comes—the *What You Need to Know* series, can be used by individuals or groups for just that reason.

Here are five other reasons why we believe you will enjoy using this guide:

1. It is easy to read.

You don't want to wade through complicated technical jargon to try to stumble on the important truths you are looking for. This series puts biblical truth right out in the open. It is written in a warm and friendly style with even a smattering of humor here and there. See if you don't think it is different from anything you have ever read before.

2. It is easy to teach.

You don't have time to spend ten hours preparing for Sunday school, small group, or discipleship lessons. On the other hand, you don't want watered down material that insults your group's intellect. There is real meat in these pages, but it is presented in a way that is easy to teach. It follows a question-and-answer format that can be used to cover the material, along with discussion questions at the end of each chapter that make it easy to get group interaction going.

3. It is thoroughly biblical.

You believe the Bible, and don't want to use anything that isn't thoroughly biblical. This series has been written and reviewed by a team of people who are well-educated, personally committed Christians who have a high view of Scripture, and great care has been taken to reflect what the Bible teaches. If the Bible is unambiguous on a subject, such as the resurrection of Christ, then that subject is presented unambiguously.

4. It respectfully presents differing evangelical positions.

You don't want anyone forcing conclusions on you that you don't agree with. There are many subjects in the Bible on which there is more than one responsible position. When that is the case, this series presents those positions with respect, accuracy and fairness. In fact, to make sure, a team of evaluators from various evangelical perspectives has reviewed each of the volumes in this series.

5. It lets you follow up with your own convictions and distinctives on a given issue.

You may have convictions on an issue that you want to communicate to the people to whom you are ministering. These books give you that flexibility. After presenting the various responsible positions that may be held on a given subject, you will find it easy then to identify and expand upon your view or the view of your church

We send this study guide to you with the prayer that God may use it to help strengthen His church for her work in these days.

How To Teach This Book

The books in this series are written so that they can be used as a thirteen-week curriculum, ideal for Sunday school classes or other small-group meetings. You will notice that there are only twelve chapters—to allow for a session when you may want to do something else. Every quarter seems to call for at least one different type of session, because of holidays, summer vacation, or other special events. If you use all twelve chapters, and still have a session left in the quarter, have a fellowship meeting with refreshments, and use the time to get to know others better. Or use the session to invite newcomers in hopes they will continue with the course.

All ten books in the series together form a "Basic Knowledge Curriculum" for Christians. Certainly Christians would eventually want to know more than is in these books, but they should not know less. Therefore, the series is excellent for seekers, for new Christians, and for Christians who may not have a solid foundation of biblical education. It is also a good series for those whose biblical education has been spotty.

Of course, the books can also be used in small groups and discipleship groups. If you are studying the book by yourself, you can simply read the chapters and go through the material at the end. If you are using the books to teach others, you might find the following guidelines helpful:

Teaching Outline

1. Begin the session with prayer.

2. Consider having a quiz at the beginning of each meeting over the self-test from the chapter to be studied for that day. The quiz can be optional, or the group may want everyone to commit to it, depending on the setting in which the material is

taught. In a small discipleship group or one-on-one, it might be required. In a larger Sunday school class, it might need to be optional.

3. At the beginning of the session, summarize the material. You may want to have class members be prepared to summarize the material. You might want to bring in information that was not covered in the book. There might be some in the class who have not read the material, and this will help catch them up with those who did. Even for those who did read it, a summary will refresh their minds and get everyone into a common mind-set. It may also generate questions and discussion.

4. Discuss the material at the end of the chapters as time permits. Use whatever you think best fits the group.

5. Have a special time for questions and answers, or encourage questions during the course of discussion. If you are asked a question you can't answer (it happens to all of us), just say you don't know, but that you will find out. Then, the following week, you can open the question and answer time, or perhaps the discussion time, with the answer to the question from last week.

6. Close with prayer.

You may have other things you would like to incorporate, and flexibility is the key to success. These suggestions are given only to guide, not to dictate. Prayerfully, choose a plan suited to your circumstances.

Part One:
Understanding Spiritual Growth

The egg's no chick by falling from the hen, Nor man a Christian till he's born again.
■ John Bunyan (1628–1688)

1

When Does Spiritual Growth Begin?

A man was planting beans in his garden one spring. After plowing a shallow furrow with his hoe, he punched his finger an inch into the soft soil, put in one dried bean, moved down the furrow six inches, and planted another one, and so on down the row. He had tilled the soil until it was soft and receptive, and then fertilized the beans and watered them generously. The next couple of weeks produced weather perfect for a garden—hot days and warm nights with just enough rain at just the right times. Soon, he noticed that although most of the beans had sprouted, a number of them had not. Digging up the beans that had not sprouted, he found, to his dismay, that they were not dried beans at all, but little pebbles approximately the same size and color of the beans he had planted. With his dimming eyesight and in his concentration over getting the job done, he had not detected the impostors. Somehow, stones had gotten into the seed beans, and quality control measures at the factory had not caught the mistake.

So, in spite of the carefully prepared soil, in spite of the water, in spite of the fertilizer, in spite of the hot days and warm nights, the pebbles never sprouted, and they never would have. Why? Because no life sparked in them to begin with. Lifeless things cannot grow. Only living things can grow.

In this chapter we learn that . . .

1. The beginning point for spiritual growth is to be spiritually born again.
2. Being in Christ means that we are joint-heirs with Him and recipients of the eternal kindness which God intends to bestow on His children.

And so it is with people, spiritually. Without God's touch giving us spiritual life, we are like human pebbles. We may receive all the spiritual food, water, and sunshine available, but we still will not grow spiritually. We must undergo the divinely initiated miracle of being changed from "pebbles" to "beans," from lifeless stone to living seed. This is precisely what God said He would do—remove our hearts of stone and give us a living heart (Ezekiel 11:19).

What Is the Beginning Point for Spiritual Growth?

The beginning point for spiritual growth is to be spiritually born again.

Because lifeless things cannot grow, a discussion of spiritual growth must begin with a look at spiritual birth. What does it mean to have a "heart of stone," and how is that stone removed?

Spiritual Death

To have a heart of stone is a metaphor for spiritual death. But what is spiritual death? The Bible says that "all have sinned and fall short of the glory of God" (Romans 3:23) and that "the wages of sin is death" (Romans 6:23). Clearly this does not mean physical death, because the apostle Paul describes people as spiritually dead who are physically alive (Ephesians 2:1). Neither is spiritual death the cessation of conscious existence nor the cessation of being, because the Bible says that people who are spiritually dead when they die will go to hell where they will experience conscious suffering (Revelation 14:9–11).

The Bible defines spiritual death. If spiritual death is not physical death or the cessation of conscious existence, then what does it mean to be spiritually dead?

Perhaps the closest we can come to a biblical explanation of spiritual death can be found by examining several passages. First, we read in Romans 5:10, "For if when we were enemies we were reconciled to God through the death of His Son, much more, having been reconciled, we shall be saved by His life." In this passage, we see that to be spiritually dead (Romans 6:23) means to be an "enemy" of God, to be "unreconciled" to God.

We read also in Colossians 1:21–22, "And you, who once were alienated and enemies in your mind by wicked works, yet now He has reconciled in the body of His flesh through death, to present you holy, and blameless, and above reproach in His sight." In this passage, spiritual death is a condition of being alienated from God because of sin (Romans 3:23).

So we can conclude from these passages that spiritual death means "to be in a state of alienation and unreconciliation from God because of sin."

In this unreconciled state, we are cut off from His temporal blessings as well as His eternal blessings. His temporal blessings include His loving providence in our lives, His leading and guidance, and the general blessings which He bestows on His children. His eternal blessings, of course, include the gift of eternal life, fellowship with Him, and a place in heaven. Without those blessings, we are in dire trouble. With them, we are in wonderful shape.

Spiritual Birth

The Gospel of John chapter 3 records a very important discussion between Jesus and Nicodemus, a religious leader of his day. After having heard Jesus speak, Nicodemus came to Jesus by night. Some have speculated that he came by night to avoid detection, since it would not have been a politically popular meeting for him among his fellow Pharisees. He said to Jesus, "Rabbi, we know that you are a teacher come from God; for no one can do these signs that You do unless God is with him" (v. 2).

Jesus did not respond directly to that statement. Rather, He zeroed in on what He saw as the real issue in Nicodemus' life. He said, "Most assuredly, I say to you, unless one is born again, he cannot see the kingdom of God" (v. 3).

Nicodemus said, in effect, "Why, how in the world is a man going to be born again? He cannot re-enter his mother's womb a second time and be born again, can he?"

Jesus Himself introduced the startling concept of being born again.

Of course, Nicodemus, not being a biological ignoramus, clearly knew that that was impossible. It was a rhetorical question. Jesus responded, "Most assuredly, I say to you, unless one is born of water and of the Spirit, he cannot enter the kingdom of God" (v. 5).

Theologians debate what Jesus meant by the words "water and spirit." Some contend that He meant a person had to be baptized with water in order to be saved. That is a minority position, however, among evangelicals and fundamentalists. A more common position is that the "water" refers to the amniotic fluid that breaks just before a child is born. If this is the understanding of what Jesus meant, it would be consistent with the context (Nicodemus had just asked, "Can [a person] enter a second time into his mother's womb and be born?" 3:4), and would also be a very logical comparison between a person being born once, physically, making him a member of a physical kingdom, and being born a second time, spiritually, making him a member of a spiritual kingdom.

How is a person born again? By believing in and receiving Jesus as his personal Savior. In John 1:12, the apostle wrote, "But as many as received Him, to them He gave the right to become children of God, to those who believe in His name." In this verse, we have two key words: *believe* and *receive*, which together carry the full force of what it takes to be born again. One must believe that Jesus is God (John 1:1), and must embrace Him personally (John 1:12). When that happens, at that precise moment, a person is born again, is a Christian, is destined for heaven, and is capable of spiritual growth.

Being born again moves us from being spiritually dead to being spiritually alive. Christians differ in how they view the relation of baptism to salvation. Some believe baptism follows salvation. Others believe it precedes salvation. Others view them as simultaneous. But all well-informed Christians recognize the importance of baptism as an expression of submission to the lordship of Christ. As such, baptism is an important first step in our spiritual life.

New Spirit

When a person is born again spiritually, he is, at that moment, made spiritually new. Nothing else has to happen to a person's spirit in order for that person to go to heaven. We see in Ephesians 4:24, the spirit is "created . . . in true righteousness and holiness." In Romans 7, Paul says that the "inner man," which seems to be a synonym for the spirit, does not sin (Romans 7:20), delights in the law of God (Romans 7:22), serves the law of God (Romans 7:25), and is no longer under condemnation (8:1). It only remains for the born-again spirit to be united with a new body created without sin in order for the Christian to be complete and to experience his full adoption as a child of God (Romans 8:23).

We learn from this that good people do not go to heaven. Only born-again people do. No one is good enough of themselves to get into heaven. Titus 3:5 says that we are saved, "not by works of righteousness which we have done, but according to His mercy He saved us, through the washing of regeneration and renewing of the Holy Spirit."

How good we are on earth has absolutely nothing whatsoever to do with whether or not we go to heaven, since the best person ever to have lived was not good enough to make it. And no one is so bad that he will not be forgiven and born again, if he will believe in and receive Jesus as his God and Savior.

Why I Need to Know This

If I don't understand that being born again is the determining issue as to whether or not I am a Christian, I might be deceived into thinking that I can get to heaven by being "good" (and miss it altogether), rather than by accepting Jesus as my Savior and get into heaven based on His righteousness.

Also, if I don't understand who I am in Christ, I will be limited in my ability to live like who I have become, and will miss much of the joy and meaning of the Christian life.

I used to picture this at the final judgment: God would line up all the people who had ever lived, with the worst person on the far left and the best person on the far right. Then He would count toward the middle to find the exact center of goodness in all humanity. Those on the right of that point would go to heaven, those on the left would go to hell (don't ask me where I got that concept—I have no idea).

Others have a more individual view. They imagine a set of scales being used at the final judgment. A person's good works are put on one side of the scale and his bad works are put on the other. If the good works outweigh the bad, the person goes to heaven; if not, he goes to hell. I don't know what would happen in the event that the good and bad works balanced perfectly!

Still others consider that some sins will send you to hell and other sins will not send you to hell. If you can squeak by without committing one of the whoppers, you will go to heaven. Usually only murder, child abuse, and other heinous sins are considered bad enough.

Where do we get these fanciful concepts? I have no idea. But the Bible clears up all mystery. You go to heaven if you are born again. You go to hell if you are not. You are born again when you believe in and receive Jesus as your God and Savior. And you cannot begin growing spiritually until you are born again.

Forgiveness

When we are born again, at least three things happen. First, our sins are forgiven. When we receive Christ, He forgives our sins, past, present and future, as far as our eternal destiny is concerned. Of course, sin has earthly consequences (Hebrews 12:5–11), and will influence our eternal rewards (2 Corinthians 5:10). But they will never keep us out of heaven (Romans 5:20–21). Why? Because Jesus "bore our sins in His body on the tree [cross]" (1 Peter 2:24). Because sin causes death, either we have to die, or else we have to accept Christ, who substitutes His death for ours. But if Christ has paid for our sins, we cannot pay for them. Whether or not the new Christian senses an immediate forgiveness for sins or not, he can rest on the promise of God that his sins have been blotted out. We dare to believe such an unbelievable thing because the Bible says it. Ephesians 1:7 says, "In Him [Christ] we have redemption through His blood, the forgiveness of sins, according to the riches of His grace." Then, in Ephesians 4:32 we read, "And be kind to one another, tenderhearted, forgiving one another, just as God in Christ also forgave you." Yes, the first, wonderful thing that happens to us when we are born again is that our sins are forgiven.

New Life

Second, we are given new life in Christ. Old things pass away; all things become new (2 Corinthians 5:17). We don't turn over a new leaf. Christ gives us new life. The Christian now partakes of the divine nature of Christ: "His divine power has given to us all things that pertain to life and godliness, through the knowledge of Him who called us by glory and virtue, by which have been given to us exceedingly great and precious promises, that through these you may be partakers of the divine nature" (2 Peter 1:3–4).

Holy Spirit

Third, the Holy Spirit comes to indwell the believer. Romans 8:9 says, "But you are not in the flesh but in the Spirit, if indeed the Spirit of God dwells in you. Now if anyone does not have the

Spirit of Christ, he is not His." And in 1 Corinthians 6:19 we are taught, "Or do you not know that your body is the temple of the Holy Spirit who is in you, whom you have from God, and you are not your own?"

The Spirit convicts us of sin and calls us to righteousness (John 16:8) and works in us to desire and work for God's will (Philippians 2:12–13). When we respond to His working, He creates in us a character that reflects Jesus Christ (Galatians 5:22–23).

The Church

Finally, being born again immediately places the new Christian into the body of Christ. We become part of God's family. We are not alone. The apostle Paul writes of this mystical relationship in Ephesians 2:19–22:

> Now, therefore, you are no longer strangers and foreigners, but fellow citizens with the saints and members of the household of God, having been built on the foundation of the apostles and prophets, Jesus Christ Himself being the chief cornerstone, in whom the whole building, being fitted together, grows into a holy temple in the Lord, in whom you also are being built together for a dwelling place of God in the Spirit.

The late Malcolm Muggeridge, a noted British author and editor, once wrote of his conversion to Christ:

> This is how I came to see my situation, in a sort of dream or vision; something more vivid and actual than most happenings and experiences. I am confined in the tiny dark dungeon of my ego; manacled with the appetites of the flesh, shackled with the inordinate demands of the will—a prisoner serving a life sentence with no hope of deliverance. Then I notice that high above me there is a window through which a faint flow of light comes filtering in. Seemingly so far away, so remote and inaccessible; yet I realize a window looking out onto eternity. Inside darkness, a place of fantasies and fury; outside, the white radiance of God's love shining through the universe, what the Apostle Paul called the glorious liberty of the children of God.
>
> And the window? I know what that is too—the Incarnation. Time and eternity intersecting in a cross; now becoming Always. God revealing Himself as a man, and reaching down to us, in order that we, reaching up, may relate ourselves to Him. Now I observe that the window is not, after all, far away, but near at hand, and that seen

through it everything makes sense; as it were, comes into sin, so that like the blind man whose sight Jesus restored, I can say: "One thing I know, that whereas I was blind, now I see. Thenceforth, whenever I am looking through the window, I see life as being full of joy and hope and brotherliness" (*How Christians Grow*, Russell Hitt, 19–20).

What Is the Significance of Being in Christ?

Being in Christ means that we are joint-heirs with Him and recipients of the eternal kindness which God intends to bestow on His children.

Many years ago, one of the most beautiful and popular actresses in Hollywood, Grace Kelly, left her career of superstardom to marry Prince Rainier of Monaco. Though she was certainly no stranger to fame and fortune, her life, nevertheless, underwent a dramatic change. As a result of her union with Prince Rainier, as a consequence of her "becoming one" with him, she became royalty. His royal title was now hers. His palace was now hers. His fortune was now hers. In all, his destiny was now her destiny.

And so it is with Christ. As Christians, we become the bride of Christ (Ephesians 5:22–33). As His bride, as a result of becoming one with Christ (Ephesians 5:31–32), we become royalty. Christ's life is now our life. His inheritance is now our inheritance (Ephesians 1:11), His destiny is now our destiny (Romans 8:17). The phrase "in Christ" or a related phrase occurs twenty-seven times in the Book of Ephesians alone! Being in Christ means to be one with Christ, to be fellow-travelers and fellow-heirs with Him on an eternal journey. It means being delivered from the power of darkness and translated into the kingdom of the Son of His love (Colossians 1:13).

There are two reasons why we need to understand our position in Christ. First, that position is the basis of all spiritual growth. Consider the analogy of the fruit and the vine. In John 15:5 Jesus said, "I am the vine, you are the branches. He who abides in Me, and I in him, bears much fruit; for without Me you can do nothing."

Can you imagine a bunch of grapes swelling with moisture, turn rosy then brilliant red, and producing mature, sweet fruit if that bunch of grapes has been broken off the vine? Of course not.

The very life, the nutrients, the sustenance to grow and mature depend on the grapes' attachment to the vine.

So it is with the Christian. Without Christ, we can do nothing. Without Christ we cannot grow to maturity and produce fruit. Even the apostle Paul, formidable as he was in his own right, confessed that "I have been crucified with Christ; **The Christian is born into new life in Christ.**

it is no longer I who live, but Christ lives in me; and the life which I now live in the flesh I live by faith in the Son of God, who loved me and gave Himself for me" (Galatians 2:20).

Certainly, there is much mystery in this passage, much that we do not fully understand. But one thing is clear. The apostle Paul believes that his relationship with Christ is essential to his life as a Christian.

In Romans 6:4 Paul wrote, "We were therefore buried with him through baptism into death in order that, just as Christ was raised from the dead, through the glory of the Father, we too may live a new life" (NIV). This is not talking about water baptism, but the placing of the Christian into Christ. This mystical experience has the consequence of enabling us to live a new life. Linking together the primary clauses, we read, "We were buried with him through baptism . . . in order that . . . we too may live a new life."

So, not only did Christ die for us, in some way in God's eyes, we died with Christ and rose again from the dead with Him. This does not mean that we are saved by being baptized in water, as some suggest. It means only that in some way we may not fully understand, we died and rose again in Christ when we were born again.

There is more, however. In Romans 6:6 we read, "For we know that our old self was crucified with him so that the body of sin might be done away with, that we should no longer be slaves to sin" (NIV). This crucifixion is not a present experience, but a past event. In some way, in God's eyes, we are not only crucified with Christ but we are also resurrected with Him when we are born again.

Because of this Paul tells us to "consider ourselves dead to sin but alive to God" (v. 14).

All of this was decided before we were ever born. "He [God] chose us in Him [Christ] before the foundation of the world, that we should be holy and without blame before Him" (Ephesians

1:4). Our union with Jesus, our identification with Him in the eyes of God, our mysterious crucifixion and resurrection with Him—this is the basis by which we can accept by faith that we have died to sin and have come alive to God. **The Christian is dead to sin but alive unto God.** This does not mean that we never again sin. It does mean that we no longer belong to sin. Sin no longer owns us. The legal chains to sin, which would require our spiritual death, have been broken.

Paul gives an example in Romans 7:1–6. The law has dominion over a man as long as he lives, Paul argues. But if he dies, obviously, the law no longer rules him. Then Paul gives the example of a husband and wife. The woman is bound to her husband as long as the husband lives, but when the husband dies, she is no longer bound to him, and she is free to remarry.

Like a husband and wife were married for life until one of them died, so we and sin were married for life. We were bound to our husband (sin) as long as we lived. But when we died in Christ, we were no longer legally bound to sin, and were free to remarry righteousness. So we may sin in our daily lifestyle, but we are no longer bound to sin. "Sin shall no longer have dominion over you," Paul writes in Romans 6:14. Because of that, we can stop presenting ourselves to sin as instruments of unrighteousness, and can instead present ourselves to God as instruments of righteousness.

The Christian lifestyle is possible, progressive, and powerful. This lifestyle is not automatic, but it is possible. It is not instant, but it can be progressive. When we accept this, when we believe this, when we wed this truth with other scriptural truth, it gives us greater power to live like who we have become—children of God, created in true righteousness and holiness (Ephesians 4:24).

Since we all tend to live the way we see ourselves, it is imperative that we see ourselves as God sees us: redeemed children of celestial royalty, co-heirs with Christ, destined for the throne with Him, unchained from our marriage to sin, and capable of living progressively holy lifestyles (1 Peter 1:15–16). "As the twig is bent, so grows the tree," says the proverb. Things that happen to us when we are young often direct the course of our lives. But they don't have to. Christ can change the bend. He can straighten the trunk. He can prune the wayward branches and make of us a beautiful, healthy, stretching heavenward tree.

Part of this process is believing that we really are who the Bible says we are in Christ. If we see ourselves as worms, we will tend to act like worms. Acting like worms will hold back our spiritual growth. If we see ourselves as children of a king, we will tend to act like princes and princesses. Acting like royalty will advance our spiritual growth.

Surely, sin in the flesh (Romans 7:14—8:1) holds us back from perfect fulfillment on earth of our ultimate destiny, but let us not forget our ultimate destiny. God originally created humanity in His image. That creation was thwarted when sin entered the human race through Adam and Eve's rebellion. But God is going to restore us to His perfect image, and will do so in Christ. The basis of this reconciliation is our union with Christ, the foundation of all spiritual growth.

"But we all, with unveiled face, beholding as in a mirror the glory of the Lord, are being transformed into the same image from glory to glory, just as by the Spirit of the Lord" (2 Corinthians 3:18). Those linked with Christ will

> **The Christian has the promise of being restored to God's perfect image.**

demonstrate growing Christlike qualities here on earth, and one day will be transformed fully into His likeness.

Of course, we don't always feel very Christlike. We see the hidden lust, the secret surges of selfishness and pride, the flashes of anger or the smoldering envy. Aware of our commitment to self-determination, self-protection, and self-gratification, we know our own hearts. But God knows our frame. He is mindful that we are but dust (Psalm 103:14) and takes care of that now. "If we confess our sins, He is faithful and just to forgive us our sins and to cleanse us from all unrighteousness" (1 John 1:9). And eventually we will stand before Him, rid of these sin-corrupted bodies, never to sin again (Romans 8:23).

Conclusion

Imagine that you were born the child of the king and queen of a rich and powerful nation. However, shortly after your birth, a hoodlum who hated your mother and father kidnapped you in the middle of the night and spirited you away to a country on a faraway continent. There, you were sold as a slave to a niggardly, dishonest, and evil man. As you grew up, he treated you like dirt, called you ugly names, dressed you in rags, and forced you to live his evil lifestyle of crime and degradation. You had no idea you were the child of a king and heir to a fabulous fortune. You had no concept of the fact that, if you were in your rightful home, you would be treated like the royalty you really were. You saw yourself only as the child of a thief.

However, you had a distinct birthmark on your left temple— a small red patch of skin shaped somewhat like a wildflower. Your evil "father" told you it was the curse of the devil. You believed him.

One day, the king's chief steward came to that faraway country to trade. He brought gold and silver with which to buy silk, spices, and exotic foods. Lurking in a corner of the marketplace, your fingers itching for an opportunity to grab that bag of gold, you looked up to find the steward's eyes fixed on the birthmark on your left temple. He stared hard at you, his mind racing, not yet daring to believe what he saw. That birthmark, so distinctive! The age, just right! Could it be?

You went cold at his scrutiny. Why was he looking at you? Did he know your evil deeds? Was he plotting your capture and imprisonment? Before you can escape, the steward's guards seize you and whisk you away to a room above a tavern. There, asking you many questions about yourself which you feel compelled to answer, the steward concluded who you were and told you. You were the child of a king in a faraway land. You were fabulously wealthy, had great power, great honor, and had a great future ahead of you.

Your mind reeled. You did not believe him. But any other kind of life would be better than the one you were living. You boarded his ship, which sailed immediately for home. During the long voyage the steward told you more and more about yourself. Slowly, as he put the pieces of your life puzzle together, you began to believe him. But it was difficult. You knew nothing of the values, attitudes, habits, and actions of royalty. You knew only the values, attitudes, habits, and actions of a thief.

Finally, you landed on the shores of home. The news was sped to your mother and father, who were overwhelmed. They stood ready to restore you immediately to your position as heir to their throne, but you were so twisted into another shape, you could not accept the life that awaited you. You could not accept their love. You did not even know them. You did not know how to love and be loved. Your whole life had been geared to stealing enough just to eat. Now, you had more wealth than it was possible to spend. And you had so many questions: What do you do with your time? What dreams do you dream? How do you act around the other royal people? What do you talk about—picking pockets?

Over time you learned, by observation and instruction, who you were and what your attitudes, values, habits, and actions should be. You began to acquire the mores of the kingdom. You shed the memories of the past, and dreamed of the future. It took a long time, but finally your transformation was complete. At last you stood before your mother and father, every bit the child they wanted but feared they had lost.

Of course, in this analogy, you are that child. And that is your task: To believe, accept, and re-identify with who you are; to accept the help of the King's tutors—the Holy Spirit, the Scripture, and the church; to learn the lessons of royalty; to surround yourself with those like whom you want to become; and to allow the process so to transform you that you begin to act like who you really are.

Speed Bump!

Slow down to be sure you've gotten the main points of this chapter.

Q1. What is the beginning point for spiritual growth?

A1. The beginning point for spiritual growth is to be spiritually *born again.*

Q2. What is the significance of being in Christ?

A2. Being in Christ means that we are *joint-heirs* with Him and recipients of the eternal kindness which God intends to bestow on His children.

Fill in the Blank

Q**uestion**

A**nswer**

Q1. What is the beginning point for spiritual growth?

A1. The beginning point for spiritual growth is to be spiritually _____ _____.

Q2. What is the significance of being in Christ?

A2. Being in Christ means that we are _____ - _____ with Him and recipients of the eternal kindness which God intends to bestow on His children.

For Further Thought and Discussion

1. The statement, "How good you are has nothing whatsoever to do with whether or not you go to heaven," can be a shocking statement the first time you hear it. How did you respond when you read it? Are you convinced that it is true? Why? (See Titus 3:5.)

2. Explain in your own words what it means to be a Christian. What verses in the chapter seem most important to you in coming to your understanding?

3. How well do you think you grasp who you are in Christ? How important do you think it is to have a mature grasp of that truth? Do you think you have been limited in your Christian experience by an inadequate understanding? If so, how?

What If I Don't Believe?

If I don't believe that salvation is by grace through faith in Jesus, I run the risk of missing out on heaven. I am likely to struggle with life on earth because I never know if I'm good enough to get to heaven. Also, I will lead others astray.

If I don't understand who I am in Christ, I condemn myself to limp along in the Christian life, missing out on both joy and power that comes from a proper understanding of who I am in God's eyes.

For Further Study

1. Scripture

- John 3:16
- Romans 6:4
- Romans 7:14—8:1
- 2 Corinthians 3:18
- Ephesians 1:3–14
- Ephesians 4:24
- Philippians 2:12–13
- Titus 3:5
- 1 Peter 1:15–16
- 2 Peter 1:3–4

2. Books

How to Be Born Again, Billy Graham
How Christians Grow, Russell Hitt
The Blessing, Gary Smalley and John Trent
Lifetime Guarantee, Bill Gillham

How Does God Help Me Grow Spiritually?

One of my great concerns many years ago as I was wrestling with whether or not to become a Christian was that I had "turned over new leaves" before, but they always flipped back. I had tried to be more disciplined about my study habits, I had tried to be more gracious and understanding of people who blocked my goals, and I had tried to become less enslaved to the sensual desires which assault young people in a sensual society. For a while I had some luck with each of them, but eventually I slipped back into my old thoughts, attitudes, and habits. I seemed powerless to rise above the water line of my present life.

When someone presented me with the claims of Christ and the need to give my life over to Him, I wanted to respond but feared that I would embarrass myself by "getting religion" and then relapsing as I had done with other things in my life, and as I had seen other people do with religion.

I did not understand that when one becomes a Christian, there is a "new birth" that doesn't occur when someone turns over a new leaf. New life blooms within. The very God of the universe comes to live within the new believer and works from within to keep him on track and to help keep his "leaf" turned over.

This is certainly not a perfect process. Christians respond quite imperfectly to God's living within them, but nevertheless, this indwelling differentiates "turning over a new leaf" from "gaining a new life." God lives within. We are not on our own.

A number of verses talk of each member of the Trinity indwelling the believer. The most obvious and frequent is the Holy Spirit (Romans 8:9), but Christ is also said to live within us (Colossians 1:27), as does God the Father (John 14:23; 1 John 4:4, 16).

In this chapter we learn that . . .

1. The Bible teaches that all spiritual growth begins with the work of God in my life.
2. In my spiritual life, God makes it possible for me gradually to know, become, and do everything He requires of me.
3. I balance my spiritual life by actively pursuing spiritual growth while resting in the fact that God alone gives spiritual growth.
4. I cope with failure by accepting that while God wants me to grow spiritually, He knows I will often fail, and so does not demand perfect behavior from me.

This is a remarkable fact. No other religion in the world makes such a claim. Russell Hitt, in his book *How Christians Grow*, writes,

> I have made several trips to Asia, and I have met a number of Buddhists. We have talked about Buddhism on a number of occasions but never once have I heard a Buddhist say that the great Siddhartha Gautama was some-how living inside him. My Asian friends would be polite in true Oriental fashion but they would think I was insane if I were to ask if the Buddha was in any sense personally present within them. But Christianity teaches just such an astounding truth (30).

This is, of course, why becoming a Christian is more than turning over a new leaf. This indwelling God sovereignly works within us to live new lives which reflect the spiritual rebirth within.

What Does the Bible Teach About My Spiritual Growth?

The Bible teaches that all spiritual growth begins with the work of God in my life.

Sanctification (the theological term for "spiritual growth") is "the work of God's free grace, whereby we are renewed in the whole man after the image of God, and are enabled more and more to die unto sin, and live unto righteousness" (*Westminster Shorter Catechism*, Q.35).

This is indeed what happens to us. Because when we are born again God lives within, and because He renews us from within to enable us more and more to die to sin and live righteously, becoming a Christian is more than turning over a new leaf. It is transformation into a whole new life.

God works first to bring us to Himself. He initiates the search.

This is true not only in spiritual growth but also in the initial process of becoming a Christian. God initiates. He works first. We respond. It is as someone said, "I looked and looked for God and when I found Him, I learned that it was He who had found me."

We see an example of this in the life of C. S. Lewis, the British intellect who became one of Christendom's most articulate spokesmen. He taught at both Oxford and Cambridge Universities during his academic career. The story of his spiritual journey from atheist to agnostic to Christian is a heartening one. In his book, *Surprised by Joy*, he wrote:

Early in 1926, the hardest boiled of all the atheists I ever knew sat in my room on the other side of the fire and remarked that the evidence for the [historical accuracy] of the Gospels was really surprisingly good. "Rum thing," he went on. "All that stuff of Frazer's about the Dying God. Rum thing. It almost looks as if it had really happened once." To understand the shattering impact of [that statement] you would need to know the man (who has certainly never since shown any interest in Christianity). If he, the cynic of cynics, the toughest of the toughs, were not—as I would still have put it—"safe," where could I (who was doing constant intellectual battle with it) turn? Was there no escape? (228)

Finally, the intellectual reality pressed down on him so completely that he began to yield.

You must picture me alone in [my room at Cambridge] night after night, feeling, whenever my mind lifted even for a second from my work, the steady, unrelenting approach of Him whom I so earnestly desired not to meet. That which I greatly feared had at last come upon me. In the Trinity term of 1929 I gave in, and admitted that God was God, and knelt and prayed: perhaps, that night, the most dejected and reluctant convert in all England. I did not then see what is now the most shining and obvious thing; the Divine humility which will accept a convert even on such terms. The Prodigal Son at least walked home on his own feet. But who can duly adore that Love which will open the high gates to a prodigal who is brought in kicking, struggling, resentful, and darting his eyes in every direction for a chance of escape? The words, in the Gospels, "compel them to come in,". . . . properly understood, plumb the depths of the Divine mercy.

The hardness of God is kinder than the softness of men, and His compulsion is our liberation. (229)

Lewis experienced the work of God in drawing him to Christ, and the work of God in leading him to a life of righteousness in the ensuing years. But it is also important to note that Lewis also responded. It is not all one way. Like each wing of an airplane, the work of God and the work of the individual must both play a role. But it begins with God. A number of passages point this out.

Why I Need to Know This

If I think that too much of the Christian life is up to me, I will be frustrated and defeated at my inability to measure up. On the other hand, if I think that too much of the Christian life is up to God, I may not put forth the effort required of me to grow spiritually. Finally, I need to know this so that when I fail, I will not fall into the trap of thinking God has abandoned me.

In Philippians 2:12–23, Paul admonishes us to "work out your own salvation with fear and trembling; for it is God who works in you both to will and to do for His good pleasure."

In 1 Corinthians 3:6 we see a similar concept where the apostle Paul wrote, "I planted, Apollos watered, but God gave the increase." Yes, people may minister and be ministered to, but God produces spiritual results.

In a companion passage, we learn that salvation begins with a work of God: "No man can come to me unless the Father who sent me draws him" (John 6:44).

We learn also that spiritual growth is a work of the Holy Spirit: "The fruit of the Spirit is love, joy, peace, patience, kindness, goodness, faithfulness, gentleness, self-control" (Galatians 5:22–23).

Finally, we read in John 15:5: "I am the vine, you are the branches. He who abides in Me, and I in him, bears much fruit; for without Me you can do nothing."

So there we have it—the unambiguous and abundant testimony that our spiritual birth and spiritual growth begins with God.

What Does God Do For Me in My Spiritual Life?

In my spiritual life, God makes it possible for me gradually to know, become, and do everything He requires of me.

There is an old saying:

> *God does the work of God,*
> *Man does the work of Man*;*
> *Man cannot do the work of God,*
> *God will not do the work of Man.*

We must understand what God's work is and what our work is. God works in our lives, from the inside out, to transform us into His image. The process is not a perfect one. We rebel. We misunderstand. We fail. Nevertheless, God is always with us and will never forsake us. He is always there, calling, guiding, comforting strengthening, enlightening. Although we respond imperfectly, God nudges us closer and closer to the kind of person He wants us to be.

Why the process doesn't work any better than it does, I don't know. All of us wish we could be better Christians. And even while we are wishing it, we sometimes knowingly do things we shouldn't. But God is faithful, and will not reject us, even when we, His born-again children, may sometimes resist Him (Hebrews 12:5–11).

God helps us grow spiritually in several ways. This short list is not complete. He does many more things than this, but these three major things will aid us in understanding His work in our lives.

God Illuminates Our Minds to Understand Truth

The apostle Paul makes it very clear in 1 Corinthians 2 that the unregenerate person does not have the innate ability to understand or willingness to embrace the truth of Scripture: "But the natural man does not receive the things of the Spirit of God, for they are foolishness to him; nor can he know them, because they are spiritually discerned" (v. 14). We do not naturally receive or understand the spiritual truth revealed to us in the Scripture. But

* (humanity. male and female)

when we become a Christian, the indwelling God illumines our mind to know them increasingly: "But God has revealed them [spiritual truths] to us through His Spirit" (v. 10).

I will never forget the torment I experienced just before becoming a Christian. I got out our huge family Bible and tried to read it. I could have made more sense out of the phone book. I remembered nothing. However, the day after I became

The Spirit of God kindles the Word of God to enlighten us.

a Christian, someone gave me a paperback New Testament and encouraged me to read the Gospel of John six times as soon as I could. I did. I couldn't get enough of it. I didn't understand everything, but I thrilled in what I did understand, and was willing to wait until later for the things I didn't understand. It was certainly a newly opened book to me. The difference? The Spirit of God within kindled my mind to the Scripture and gave me an interest in, understanding of, and desire for it.

God Gives Us Godly Desires and Character

As we have already seen in Philippians 2:12–13, God works in us "both to will and to do for His good pleasure." When we want to do something for God, it is not we who are responsible for that desire, but God. We are responsible to act on it, but God put the desire there.

I remember well my pre-Christian days. Before I became a Christian after my first year in college, I wanted to graduate with a double major in business and psychology, to go into motivational research, and become an advertiser. How advertisers manipulate us, without our knowing it, into buying their products intrigued me. While I hated bad advertising, I loved good advertising. I wanted to have fun, get rich, and achieve renown in my field. That was what I wanted before I became a Christian.

The day I became a Christian, I lost those desires. How could I immerse myself in the pursuit of personal peace, prosperity, and happiness when so many people were suffering, when so many people needed Christ? It was unthinkable. I committed myself to the vocational ministry without a second backward glance.

I am not saying that advertising is wrong, or that everyone has to go into the vocational ministry if he is to be fully committed to Christ. If every Christian entered the vocational ministry, who would support pastors, missionaries, evangelists, and teachers? God does not expect or even want everyone to go into the vocational ministry. He wants most of us to honor Him in the workplace that He has given us. My story shows how God places in our hearts the desire to do His will. In this case, the vocational ministry was His will for me.

Sometimes in the process of changing our desires and character, God convicts us of sin. Before I became a Christian, I often felt smug and superior when I sinned and got away with it. I felt that I was "one up" on everyone else. While I was certainly no gangster or thug, nevertheless I had lied, cheated, and stolen with no remorse. After I became a Christian, the same kinds of activities, when I fell into them again, caused such deep remorse that I could barely function until I had confessed them and made restitution. The difference? The Spirit of God convicting me of sin, as the Scripture says He does. In John 16:8 we read, "And when He [the Holy Spirit] has come, He will convict the world of sin, and of righteousness, and of judgment."

The desire to do the will of God comes from God.

Not only was I convicted of my sin, but I also had a longing to be better than I was. I longed to be like the exemplary Christians around me. Later, I realized that it was Jesus I wanted to be like, and these exemplary Christians were signposts on the highway of life, pointing me to Him.

When we live in obedience to God's teachings, the indwelling God changes our character from our natural, unredeemed self to reflect the character of Christ while at the same time preserving the essence of our personality. In Romans 8:29, we read of God's goal for us: "For whom He foreknew, He also predestined to be conformed to the image of His Son." This transformation into the image of Jesus will not be complete until we stand before Him in heaven (Romans 8:23), yet it begins the moment we are born again. As we live and walk in the Spirit (Galatians 5:25), we are given the fruit of the Spirit (Galatians 5:22–23), which is the character of Christ.

This is another truth of Scripture which has been validated in my life. Before I was a Christian, I was dominated by self-serving inclinations. These inclinations will never be annihilated in this life, but they can be brought under the increasing control of the Holy Spirit (Romans 6:12–14)

Not only does God give us the desire to be righteous, but He strengthens us to do what is right. We have already touched on this earlier, but we read the apostle Paul's prayer for the Ephesians that God would grant them, "according to the riches of His glory, to be strengthened with might through His spirit in the inner man" (Ephesians 3:16).

This strength is often very subtle. It helps us do what is right in a given situation. It braces us to ask forgiveness from someone we have wronged. It allows us to forgive someone who has wronged us. It fortifies us to trust God for finances when our pockets are pulled inside out. It encourages us to share the gospel with others when we are naturally afraid to do so. It is not necessarily an innate talent to mesmerize others with powerful insight from Scripture or an eloquent defense of the faith. Rather, it is the power to do what Jesus would do if He were living the same life we have to live.

God Gives Us Spiritual Gifts with Which to Serve Him

We have seen that God enables us gradually to know (illumines our minds to understand truth) and to be (gives godly desires, convicts of sin, strengthens us to live correctly, etc.). Finally, God enables us to *do*. He gives each of us spiritual gifts, a supernatural ability to serve Him. And He calls on us to use our gifts in serving one another (1 Peter 4:10). He also exhorts us to do good to all men, especially to those who are of the household of faith (Galatians 6:10). He leads us and blesses us as we do good for others.

How Do I Balance My Spiritual Life?

I balance my spiritual life by actively pursuing spiritual growth while resting on the fact that God alone gives spiritual growth.

So, we must be balanced between what the Bible says God must do and what it says we must do. When carrying two weighty truths, one in each hand, the challenge is to keep the balance. Two milk buckets on a broomstick tend to slide to one side or to the other. The pitfall is to emphasize the work of man to the exclusion of the work of God, or to emphasize the work of God to the exclusion of the work of man.

In his book *True Spirituality*, Francis Schaeffer has coined the phrase "active passivity." The point is that we must be active in the pursuit of our spiritual growth, but at the same time, we passively submit to God to bring about growth in our lives. Romans 6:6, 11 says: "Our old self was crucified with Him, that the body of sin might be done away with, that we should no longer be slaves to sin. . . . Reckon yourselves to be dead indeed to sin, but alive to God in Christ Jesus our Lord."

Schaeffer paraphrases this idea as follows:

In our thoughts and lives now, we are to live as though we had already died, been to heaven, and come back again as risen. Imagine that a person has the opportunity to go to heaven and look around . . . then after ample time, come back to earth. He has seen it as a brute fact. He has been there, and looked at it, and then has come back. Would anything ever look the same to him again? It is as though he has died. It is as though he has been raised from the dead.

The constant pressure to conform to the world about us, the social pressure and every other kind of pressure of our day—surely would be broken. How could he conform to this, which is so marred, so broken, so caught up in revolution against God, so disgusting? How could he, in comparison with what he had seen?

What would the praise of the world be worth when one had stood in the presence of God? The wealth of the world, what would it look like beside the treasures of heaven? Man longs for power. But what is earthly power after one has seen the reality of heaven and the power of God? Our Christian calling is moment by moment to be dead to all things, that at this moment, we might be alive to God (42).

This is the mind-set that allows us to balance activity and passivity in our lives.

- ACTIVITY: We make all decisions in light of our death, resurrection, and return.

- PASSIVITY: We rest in the sovereignty of God—in His agenda and in His timetable.

"When we do this," Schaeffer writes, "we are now ready for the war. We are now ready to be used. We can now keep our balance" (42).

How Can I Cope with Failure?

I cope with failure by accepting that while God wants me to grow spiritually, He knows I will often fail, and so does not demand perfect behavior from me.

We must maintain not only our balance in life, but our perspective also. We must understand that God is patient with us. One of the Christian's great challenges is reconciling the presence of sin and weakness in his life with the holiness of God. The serious student will sooner or later stumble over the fact that God wants him to be holy, and he is trying as hard as he can to be holy, but he is not holy.

If that is all you understand, you can come to only one conclusion: God is not pleased with you.

The serious Christian will try harder. Then he will re-assess himself, only to realize he still is not holy. So he will try harder, and harder, and harder, and harder. But he cannot keep that up.

Sooner or later, he will quit. He may do so actively, no longer trying to live the Christian life, quitting his job, divorcing his spouse, buying a sports car, and moving to the beach in southern California. Or he may quit passively, continuing to go through all the motions on the outside but giving up on the inside.

This is so sad because it is unnecessary. God knows we will fail. He knows we will live imperfect lives.

One of my favorite passages in all the Bible is Psalm 103:8–14, which reads:

> The Lord is compassionate and gracious,
> Slow to anger and abounding in lovingkindness.
> He will not always strive with us;
> Nor will He keep His anger forever.
> He has not dealt with us according to our sins,
> Nor rewarded us according to our iniquities.
> For as high as the heavens are above the earth,
> So great is His lovingkindness toward those who fear Him.
> As far as the east is from the west,
> So far has He removed our transgressions from us.
> Just as a father has compassion on his children,
> So the Lord has compassion on those who fear Him.
> For He Himself knows our frame;
> He is mindful that we are but dust. (NASB)

The Lord has compassion on those who fear Him. If you are trying to live the Christian life the best way you know how but you keep stumbling and falling, God does not get sick and tired of you. He knows that you will require time to grow, and He will be patient with you. If you are not living in willful rebellion against God, then God is satisfied with you even with the weaknesses and sins in your life. If He is satisfied, then you can be satisfied.

Having said that, let me clarify what I mean by saying some things that I don't mean.

1. I don't mean that God doesn't care if you sin. He does. He wants you to be holy. He knows that sin hurts you, and He loves you—so He hates sin. But He takes into account your weaknesses. He loves you unconditionally even with the sin.

2. It doesn't mean you don't have to be concerned about sin and weakness. You do. You must be willing to repent from sin when He convicts you of it. You need to be in relationship with God for the purpose of growth through the sin and weakness.

3. The fruit of the Spirit is the fruit of the *Spirit*, not of *self-effort*, and even if you are cooperating with God the best way you know how, you do not achieve instant maturity. That means you will have to take time to grow through some of your weaknesses that you have right now because God has not done the work of grace yet to free you of them. So you must be willing to accept yourself even with the weaknesses, because God does.

Parenthetically, God deals very harshly with rebellion. He deals decisively with someone who knows what the right thing to do is, but doesn't care, or makes no attempt to do it. But He deals compassionately with weaknesses.

So we see that God is patient with our weaknesses. On that basis, we must be patient with ourselves.

Spiritual growth takes time. Be patient with yourself—and God.

To highlight what I perceive to be the importance of this truth, allow me a personal illustration. I became a Christian while a student in college, and I immediately threw myself into living the Christian life with great zeal. However, in spite of my zeal, I found myself riddled with the same inconsistencies and failures which had plagued me before I became a Christian. I remember very distinctly praying one day, "God if You want me to be holy, and if I want to be holy, then I have one question for You. Why am I not holy?"

I knew that somehow God saw me as holy and righteous through the Cross, but I was struggling with personal righteousness on a daily level. Finally I decided that I was not trying hard enough. I was not reading my Bible or praying enough to achieve the spiritual progress I longed for. So I began to read my Bible for an hour a day and to pray for another hour a day. I continued that practice for the remainder of the semester. And at the end of that semester, I was never more out of fellowship at any other time in my life.

I would get angry or selfish and do things I knew I shouldn't. When I came to my senses, I would repent. I wanted to not be angry, I wanted to not be proud, and although I worked against these emotions in my good moments, when the wrong person or circumstance confronted me, bingo! Off I would go again.

I came to hate myself. I would sin and then repent, sin and repent. "O God, I'm sorry. Help me not to do that again." Then I'd repeat the same sin and the same prayer. "O God, I'm sorry. I won't do that again." But I would. "O God, I said I wouldn't sin again, and I did. I'm sorry, but I *promise* I won't do it again." Then I'd sin again, and again, and again. Each time I asked God to help me, strengthen me. Each time I failed.

I finally was too embarrassed to come to God again. I was angry at Him for not coming to my rescue and disappointed in Him for not giving me more strength. I wanted to do right; I just couldn't seem to pull it off. At last I said, "Okay, God, I quit. I have done my absolute best, and it isn't good enough, so I quit. If You ever want to do anything with my life, just let me know, but until You do, see You later. I've had it."

Properly understood, God's grace *never* encourages us to sin.

I quit reading my Bible. I quit praying. Though I kept up appearances on the outside, on the inside I was defeated. I lived for the next two years a frustrated, defeated, angry young man. No one had ever told me that I couldn't do it all myself. No one had ever told me that I couldn't do it all immediately. No one had ever explained to me that because I was in Christ, God was satisfied with me, even with my sins, and that He recognized weaknesses and accepted me anyway because of Christ, and that therefore I could accept myself.

If someone had told me that, it wouldn't have made me want to run out and start sinning like crazy. It would have made me drop to my knees in gratitude to God for His grace. It would have been such a relief! It would have given me strength to keep on trying. Properly understood, God's grace *never* encourages us to sin. It only ever encourages us to righteousness.

A breakthrough came when I went to seminary and one of my seminary professors in theology class said, "Be patient with yourself. You can't be holy in a hurry!" My heart jumped! My mind swelled with hope. And as I stepped from a context of legalism to a context of grace, my true spiritual development began.

Conclusion

I believe that all of the wondrous things in our physical world are designed to illustrate great spiritual truths. The infinite size of the universe pictures the infinity of God. The transition from summer to fall to winter to spring models death, burial, and resurrection. Humans grow up physically the way they do for the purpose of typifying spiritual birth and spiritual growth.

A child is born utterly helpless and knowing very little. He needs constant care and attention from a loving provider. As the baby grows, we take into account age-level characteristics, and accept behavior which is not ideal, but which is normal.

If a six-month-old child wants you to hold it, and then squirms around in your lap and spits up on your shoulder, you do not consider that ideal behavior. You wish that he hadn't done it, but you accept it because the baby is only six months old. But if a thirty-year-old person squirmed around in your lap and spit up on your shoulder, you'd want an explanation!

The six-month-old child grows for six more months, and he is ready to take his first step. He takes one death-defying step, weaves dangerously to the right, spins around ninety degrees, and collapses to the floor. You don't say, "Listen you rotten kid, if you are gonna walk, walk! And if you're gonna sit down, then sit down. But stop this up-and-down business ' On the contrary

You probably have a spontaneous celebration. Whoops and handclapping and "attababy's" fill the air. Then you prop the wobbler up and encourage him to take another step, even though you know he is going to fall down again.

Falling down isn't ideal behavior, but you expect it from the age of the child. You focus, not on the fall, but on the step.

And take the child who wants to be a basketball player. He feels as though he will never grow up. Each day he begs you to measure him to see if he has gotten any taller. You know he hasn't—he hasn't had time enough to grow. But he pleads so earnestly that you humor him anyway.

The same thing is true of spiritual growth. It takes time. How much time? It depends on a million variables. But it almost always takes more time than you think it should. God will mature you, however, if you will grow His way.

So don't live in rebellion. God will deal decisively with that. Live earnestly for the Lord, accept that you can't be holy in a hurry, and give God and yourself time. In the meantime, accept yourself, because God does.

Speed Bump!

Slow down to be sure you've gotten the main points of this chapter.

Question Answer

Q1. What does the Bible teach about my spiritual growth?

A1. The Bible teaches that all spiritual growth *begins* with the work of God in my life.

Q2. What does God do for me in my spiritual life?

A2. In my spiritual life, God makes it *possible* for me gradually to know, become, and do everything He requires of me.

Q3. How do I balance my spiritual life?

A3. I balance my spiritual life by actively pursuing spiritual growth while resting in the fact that *God* alone gives spiritual growth.

Q4. How can I cope with failure?

A4. I cope with failure by accepting that while God wants me to grow spiritually, He knows I will often fail, and so does not demand *perfect* behavior from me.

Fill in the Blank

Question   **Q1.** What does the Bible teach about my spiritual
                growth?

Answer   **A1.** The Bible teaches that all spiritual growth
                _____ with the work of God in my life.

Q2. What does God do for me in my spiritual life?

A2. In my spiritual life, God makes it _____ for me gradually to
know, become, and do everything He requires of me.

Q3. How do I balance my spiritual life?

A3. I balance my spiritual life by actively pursuing spiritual growth while
resting in the fact that _____ alone gives spiritual growth.

Q4. How can I cope with failure?

A4. I cope with failure by accepting that while God wants me to grow
spiritually, He knows I will often fail, and so does not demand
_____ behavior from me.

For Further Thought and Discussion

1. If it is true that all spiritual growth originates with God, what should
our response be?

2. If God makes it possible for me to know, become, and do what He
requires of me, what do I think is the next step He wants me to take in
each of those three areas?

3. Do you have a harder time working for your spiritual growth, or
waiting on God to grant it to you? Explain.

4. When you learn that God does not demand perfect behavior from you,
does it make you want to be spiritually careless or spiritually diligent?
Explain.

What If I Don't Believe?

If I don't believe that spiritual growth is a cooperative effort between
God and me, I may become imbalanced, either putting too little emphasis on
myself or too little on God. By recognizing the cooperative nature of spiritual

growth, I can chart a course for spiritual growth that will help me be responsible for what I can do and patient for what God must do.

If I don't believe that God does not demand perfect behavior from me, I may drive myself to frustration and defeat by trying to become perfect, but not being able to.

For Further Study

1. Scripture

- Psalm 103:8–14

- 1 Corinthians 3:6

- Philippians 2:12–13

2. Books

How Christians Grow, Russell Hitt
True Spirituality, Francis Schaeffer

For all your days prepare
And meet them all alike:
When you are the anvil, bear—
When you are the hammer, strike.
■ **Edwin Markham (1852–1940)**

3

What Must I Do to Grow Spiritually?

In his autobiography, Benjamin Franklin writes about his attempt to become morally perfect. He selected thirteen qualities that he felt embodied moral perfection. He decided to work on one quality for a week to perfect it, then move to the second quality the second week to perfect it, then the third, fourth, and so on. At the end of thirteen weeks, he expected to be morally perfect.

At the end of the thirteen weeks, however, he was not yet morally perfect. So he tried again for another thirteen weeks. At the end of that time, he had still not reached the moral perfection he yearned for, so he tried again—and again, and again, and again for the rest of his life.

At the end of his life, he had to admit that he never became morally perfect. He observed very astutely, however, that though he never became morally perfect, he became a much better man for trying and failing than if he had never tried at all.

This interests us because as Christians we too long for moral perfection. That desire is a by-product of our new birth. We want to lay aside, to leave behind the sins and weaknesses of the past, and to become a whole person, to be more than we were before we came to know Christ. God then starts to work in us toward that goal.

As we saw in the last chapter, God does the work of God and man does the work of man. In the last chapter we focused on the work of God, so in this chapter we will focus on our own responsibilities.

What Are My Responsibilities in Spiritual Growth?

I must pursue mature knowledge, character, and ministry.

We saw in the last chapter that God makes it possible for us to gradually know, become, and do everything He expects of us. However, the process does not happen automatically. We must assume certain responsibilities. All of the scriptural passages we examined in the last chapter to emphasize God's role in our spiritual growth must now be turned around to see our involvement.

"Work out your own salvation with fear and trembling; for it is God who works in you, both to will and to do for His good pleasure" (Philippians 2:12–13).

God works in us to will His will and to do it, yet we have a responsibility to "work out our own salvation." This does not mean that we have to do good works to get saved or stay saved. Rather, it means to express your salvation by progressively displaying Christian living, thus revealing the work God is doing in you. God works in us, but we must respond to that work. We can kill the new desires by lack of attention and by failure to cultivate them, or we can promote their life and growth by nurturing and feeding them.

In this chapter we learn that . . .

1. I must pursue mature knowledge, character, and ministry.
2. Our motivation for obedience to God is our love for Him who first loved us.
3. My goal in spiritual growth is to become progressively more like Christ.

In 1 Corinthians 3:6, we saw the verse written by the apostle Paul, "I planted, Apollos watered, but God gave the increase." Yes, *God* produces spiritual results, but *we* must get our hands dirty in planting and our shoulders sore from watering.

We saw also that salvation begins with a work of God: "No man can come to me unless the Father who sent me draws him," Jesus says in John 6:44. Nevertheless, we are to proclaim the gospel and persuade people (Matthew 28:19–20; 2 Corinthians 5:11).

Although spiritual growth is a work of the Holy Spirit: "the fruit of the Spirit is love, joy, peace, patience, kindness, goodness, faithfulness, gentleness, self-control" (Galatians 5:22–23), we are instructed to "walk in the Spirit" (Galatians 5:16) as a means of gaining the fruit of the Spirit.

Finally, we read in John 15:5: "I am the vine, you are the branches; he who abides in Me, and I in him, he bears much fruit; for apart from Me you can do nothing." Only as we abide in Him can we bear fruit. Our task here is simply to abide.

These passages we looked at earlier show God's initiating work in ministry, but their flip side reveals our part. While spiritual growth begins with God, it will not occur without our proper response.

Therefore, as this truth relates to our obligation to become mature in knowledge, character, and ministry, we see three sets of specific responsibilities emerge.

We Must Pursue Mature Knowledge

We must read, study, memorize, meditate upon, and obey the Bible. Ignorance is darkness; knowledge is light. Falsehood is darkness; truth is light. Disobedience is darkness; obedience is light.

The Scripture says "the entrance of Thy word bringeth light," and "Thy word is a lamp unto my feet and a light unto my path." Picture yourself groping along a path in darkness where the possibility of stumbling or getting lost is very real. The Scripture lights your feet so you can see not to stumble and illuminates your path so that you won't get lost. We cannot hope to avoid stumbling or getting lost at the crossroads unless we are shining the light of Scripture on the path of our life.

We Must Pursue Mature Character

Experiencing the will of God in our Christian character requires commitment on our part:

> I beseech you therefore, brethren, by the mercies of God, that you present your bodies a living sacrifice, holy, acceptable to God, which is your reasonable service. And do not be conformed to this world, but be transformed by the renewing of your mind, that you may prove what is that good and acceptable and perfect will of God (Romans 12:1–2).

We can get the full impact of this verse by looking at it backwards. If we want to be a living demonstration of the fact that

God's will is good, perfect, and acceptable, we must not be conformed to this world. If we don't want to be conformed to this world, we must have our mind transformed. If we want to have our mind transformed, we must present our bodies a living sacrifice to God.

Taking the next step, we see that commitment requires ongoing attention.

> Do you not know that those who run in a race all run, but only one receives the prize? Run in such a way that you may win. And everyone who competes in the games exercises self-control in all things. They then do it to receive a perishable wreath, but we an imperishable. Therefore I run in such a way, as not without aim; I box in such a way, as not beating the air; but I buffet my body and make it my slave, lest possibly, after I have preached to others, I myself should be disqualified (1 Corinthians 9:24–27, NASB).

Here the apostle Paul indicates that spiritual goals (not without aim) and self-discipline (make my body my slave) present a biblical mandate for personal commitment to growth.

Why I Need to Know This

I need to know this so that I will know what I am supposed to do to encourage my own spiritual growth, which means becoming like Christ. When I understand the level on which God wants me to be obedient to Him, I can aspire to the level of obedience out of love.

In addition to our total commitment and ongoing attention to growth, we must pray. We pray not because God needs our prayers. Rather, He wants our hearts. He can gain our heart by requiring our prayer. God wants to live in close fellowship with us, and prayer encourages that fellowship. Because a relationship with God is the real motive for praying, we must resist the temptation to view God as merely a heavenly "answer" machine. To help us in that regard, God sometimes does not answer our prayers the way we want, or if He does He delays His answer. If prayers are answered easily, then we tend to treat God as a vending machine—request in, answer out—and the extent of our relationship with God is little more than regarding Him as a slot for quarters. If the product doesn't come out, we kick or shake the machine and scream that it ate our money. In this scenario, God serves man, rather than man serving God.

A third obvious thing we must do is worship the Lord. In the Gospel of John, we read that God seeks those who will worship Him in spirit and in truth (John 4:24). In Psalm 147:1 we read, "Praise the Lord! For it is good to sing praises to our God; For it is pleasant, and praise is beautiful."

Finally, we are to develop a rich community with others who are committed to the Lord. We are not designed to be able to make it alone. We need a support group, a place where we can belong. We need the church and the church needs us.

These things we must do to pursue mature character. Now we turn our attention to our third responsibility.

We Must Pursue Ministry Skills

In addition to learning what we should know and becoming what we should be, we must learn to do what we should do. We have each been given a spiritual gift by God (1 Peter 4:10) which we are to use in ministering to one another. Also, God requires us to do good to all men, especially to fellow believers (Galatians 6:10). Exercising our spiritual gifts and doing good to others is not always a simple or easy thing, however. We must work at our jobs until we can do them well.

Reading your Bible, praying, going to church, memorizing Scripture, sharing your faith with others, and helping others are good things, but in and of themselves they are insufficient. We all know people who do these things whose lives do not draw us to Christ. They have no compelling spiritual reality that creates in us a thirst to know God better. And worse, sometimes they are cold, rigid, distant, and legalistic. They do not draw us to Christ; they repel us away from Him. There is no magic in merely fulfilling these responsibilities. A chapter a day doesn't keep the devil away.

Our attitude and our perspective as we pursue God are all-important. Attitude and perspective can keep us from assembly line motions without any spiritual reality. We now turn our attention to our fundamental motivation.

What Is Our Motivation for Obedience to God?

Our motivation for obedience to God is our love for Him who first loved us.

None of us would be attracted to a church named "Boring Bible Church" or "Stoics-for-Jesus Fellowship or 'The Grin-

and-Bear-It Community Church," or "First Church of the Frozen Chosen." Yet we invite that very danger when we talk of obedience to God without understanding our motivation. There are several reasons to obey God.

First, if we don't obey God, we will pay a dreadful price. For example, if we disobey His ultimate command to believe in and receive Jesus as our personal Savior, we will be eternally condemned. If we violate His commands on lifestyle matters, we may suffer dreadful cause-effect consequences (Proverbs 6:24–29). If we are a child of God and continue in sin, we risk bringing down God's chastening hand on our lives (Hebrews 12:5–11). The Book of Hebrews says "It is a fearful thing to fall into the hands of the living God" (10:31), and "our God is a consuming fire" (12:29). We should obey God because we may well suffer for it if we don't.

But God does not leave it there. He does not want us to obey Him merely to escape punishment or negative consequences. God has other, higher reasons for requiring our obedience.

Second, God wants us to obey Him because we see the wisdom of His commands. First John 5:3 states that "His commands are not burdensome." Psalm 19 states that the law of the Lord is perfect, restoring the soul; the testimony of the Lord is sure, making wise the simple; the statutes of the Lord are right, rejoicing the heart; the commandment of the Lord is pure, enlightening the eyes, and that these are to be desired more than gold, that they are sweeter than honey (vv. 7–8, 10). The Psalmist

The wise person keeps the Word of God.

writes, "By them Your servant is warned, and in keeping them there is great reward" (v. 11). The entire Book of Proverbs is dedicated to showing the wisdom of keeping the word of God. Everything that God asks of us, He does so to give something good to us or to keep some harm from us. That is a wonderful motivation to obey God.

However, we experience the highest motivation to obey God when His love so moves us that we reciprocate. We love Him because He first loved us. We obey because we honor Him so highly and want to please Him.

Any parent easily understands this. No parents want their children to obey merely to escape punishment. However, if the child will obey for no other reason, it is still better to obey than to disobey.

Take, for example, the command of a parent for his child not to play in the street. The parent may wish that the child would obey him out of love and respect for his character and their relationship. If obedience does not occur on that level, the parent may wish that the child would obey him because the child can see the wisdom of the command. But if the child does not obey the parent on those two levels, the parent is still glad that the child obeys for the lowest level, merely to escape parental punishment, for in doing so the child avoids the danger of being run over by a car. And because of the love the parent has for the child, that level of obedience is better than no obedience. So it is with God.

I heard a story one time, which was told as a true story, about a little boy whose sister needed a blood transfusion. The blood was difficult to match, and after some investigation, it was discovered that the little boy had the same rare blood.

So the doctor asked the little boy if he would give his blood to his sister. The youngster hesitated, obviously going through a deep inner struggle. Finally he replied, "Yes. For my sister, I will."

The two children were soon wheeled into the hospital room where the transfusion was to take place. As the needle was inserted into his arm, the little boy was calm but sober. He watched the blood flow through the tube into his sister's body.

When it was almost over, the little boy asked in a quiet voice, "Doctor, when do I die?"

Only then did anyone realize that the child thought that giving his blood to save his sister would mean that he would die. What a decision! What a gift of love! What a tribute to the power of their relationship!

On that same level God asks us to give our lives to Him in faithful obedience. He wants us to yield ourselves, not with tight lips and clenched jaws of resentment and defeat, but out of love and devotion to Him. When we do, we discover that, like the little boy, we don't die. In fact, we become more alive at that moment than we have ever been before.

What Is My Goal in Spiritual Growth?

My goal in spiritual growth is to become progressively more like Christ.

Someone once said that the essence of sin is selfishness and the essence of righteousness is selflessness. In a closely related idea, C. S. Lewis once said, "Pride is the mother hen under which all other sins are hatched." Our goal in spiritual growth is to become like Christ, which means that we give up our "right" to self-determination, self-protection, and self-gratification, and we give ourselves to God and others.

Jesus stated specifically what our goal was when He was asked what was the greatest commandment. His response contained not only the greatest command, but also the second greatest:

> "You shall love the Lord your God with all your heart, with all your soul, and with all your mind." This is the first and great commandment. And the second is like it: "You shall love your neighbor as yourself." On these two commandments hang all the Law and the Prophets (Matthew 22:37–40).

So when we aim toward becoming like Jesus, we must love God and love our neighbors.

Defining what it means to love God and others can be difficult. We get rather confused with modern notions of what it means to love, often mistaking it for emotional involvement. So we turn to the Scriptures to guide us in understanding what it means to love God and others.

In John 15:10–11, Jesus declared, "If you keep my commandments, you will abide in My love, just as I have kept My Father's commandments and abide in His love. These things I have spoken to you, that My joy may remain in you, and that your joy may be full."

There is a link between willing obedience to God's commandments and our joy in life. While loving God surely means more than merely keeping His commandments, neverthe-less obedience to God's Word lies at the core of our love for Him. Even parents find it very troubling when their children tell them that they love them, but do not obey them. Willing obedience truly demonstrates love.

There is a link between obedience and joy.

A very enlightening passage in 1 Corinthians 13:4–7 clarifies some of what it means to love our neighbor:

> Love is patient, love is kind, and is not jealous; love does not brag and is not arrogant, does not act unbecomingly; it does not seek its own, is not provoked, does not take into account a wrong suffered, does not rejoice in unrighteousness, but rejoices with the truth;

bears all things, believes all things, hopes all things, endures all things (NASB).

We can gain a very uncomfortable picture of how well we love others by reading this passage out loud, substituting our name for the word *love:*

Max is patient, Max is kind, and is not jealous; Max does not brag and is not arrogant, does not act unbecomingly; he does not seek his own, is not provoked, does not take into account a wrong suffered, [Max] does not rejoice in unrighteousness, but [he] rejoices with the truth; bears all things, believes all things, hopes all things, endures all things (NASB).

If you feel perfectly comfortable doing that, you are either a saint or a calloused sinner. If it makes you squirm a little, then you are pretty normal like most of the rest of us. It helps us see more clearly ways in which we can be more loving toward others, and in doing so, be more like Jesus.

Chuck Swindoll once related Shel Silverstein's story called *The Giving Tree*, about a tree that loved a boy.

When the boy was young, he swung from the tree's branches, climbed all over her, ate her apples, slept in her shade. Such happy, carefree days. The tree loved those years.

But as the boy grew, he spent less and less time with the tree. "Come on, let's play," invited the tree on one occasion, but the young man was interested only in money. "Take my apples and sell them," said the tree. He did, and the tree was happy.

He didn't return for a long time, but the tree smiled when he passed one day. "Come on, let's play!" But the man was older and tired of his world. He wanted to get away from it all. "Cut me down. Take my large trunk and make yourself a boat. Then you can sail away," said the tree. He did, and the tree was happy.

Many seasons passed—summers and winters, windy days and lonely nights—and the tree waited. Finally, the old man returned, too old and tired to play, to pursue riches, or to sail the seas. "I have a pretty good stump left, my friend. Why don't you just sit down here and rest?" said the tree. He did, and the tree was happy (quoted in *Stories for the Heart*, compiled by Alice Gray, 126).

While the story has a sadness to it, the point for us is the spirit of giving exhibited by the tree. God has given and given and given to us, often with little more gratitude from us than the man in the story gave the tree. God so loved the world that He gave His only Son to die for our sins. Love gives. God is love, and His love gives and gives. When we truly become partakers of the nature of God, we become givers also. Through obedience, we take on the character of Christ.

What Is the Danger in Pursuing Spiritual Growth?

The danger in pursuing spiritual growth is that we try to find spiritual satisfaction our way instead of God's way.

We are always in a danger of trying to get the right thing in the wrong way. The old saying, "I want patience, and I want it *now!*" comes to mind. One cannot demand patience, or get it instantly. One can only get patience God's way by relinquishing a demanding spirit and trusting in God's inner work and timetable. Like so many things in the Christian life, you must "give up" in order to "get."

So it is with spiritual growth. We can neither demand it nor manipulate God into giving it to us ahead of schedule or in an easier way. And we cannot produce it with our own effort. But that doesn't keep many of us from trying. Many of us have deep longings that we want fulfilled and very real pain that we want to go away. If we think we can tweak things to get what we want, we are often not opposed to trying it.

Many of us yearn for a sense of self-worth and of being loved unconditionally. We long for deep, intimate relationships with God and other people. And we desire our life to count for something good. The truth is that God loves us unconditionally and calls us to a life of supreme importance in fulfilling the great commission and furthering His kingdom.

However, many of us try to get these longings fulfilled from the world around us rather than from the God within us. In doing so, we are pursuing right things in the wrong way. We give and receive love so imperfectly that we often do not have the depth of relationship that we long for with God or with people. And we are so limited in our time, our talents, and our treasures, that we do not sense the importance and worth in what we accomplish with our lives.

Therefore, we are tempted to try to manipulate God and people to give us a greater sense of loving and being loved, and we are enticed to engineer circumstances to make us look important. In short, we try to take life into our own hands and meet our own needs.

We think, *Oh, if I only had that job, or that house, or that car, or that girlfriend, or that spouse, or that bank account, or that whatever-it-is, I would be happy.* Then we get what we most wanted, and are satisfied for a while, but soon the longing comes back, and like a donkey chasing the carrot, we set off after the next thing thinking, *Well, the last thing didn't satisfy for long, but this time things will be different.* But they never are.

Only God, not the world, can satisfy our heart hungers. We continue to deceive ourselves because what we long for cannot be satisfied by things of a fallen world. What we really long for is heaven. But sometimes we lose sight of that.

So what do we do when life hurts and we scream for the pain to stop? First, we must accept life's limitations. It is okay to long. God has given us those yearnings, and has structured life so that only He can satisfy them fully or permanently. But we must be patient, we must look to Him, and we must wait for heaven.

Next, accept that it is okay to hurt. Many things in life may bring us pain: family relationships, professional circumstances, financial calamity, lost personal goals, physical pain, spiritual frustration; or more global concerns, such as moral disintegration in Western culture, famine, war, drugs, crime, prisons.

It is not unspiritual to hurt. Read the Psalms—David hurt! Read the prophets—Elijah suffered! Isaiah agonized! Jeremiah lamented! Read the Gospels—Jesus was crucified! Read the epistles—Paul was beaten! We need not paste on an artificial, wax smile. Joy and pain are not mutually exclusive.

Accept life's limitations, let the longing and let the pain drive us to God, and then rest in God's love for us. Focus our lives on the only thing that matters anyway—loving God. God's severe mercy may rip everything that we ever wanted out of our hands, but when we turn to Him with nothing left but Jesus, we find that Jesus is enough.

Most of the things I wanted out of life when I was a young man, I now realize I cannot have. When I realized that, I had a very important choice to make. I could either drop out of the ministry, get a divorce, buy a sports car, curl my hair, open my Hawaiian shirt to the navel, and start living on the beach in southern California—or I could come to grips with what really satisfies, and put all my hopes in that: loving God, loving others, and looking to heaven where all longings will be satisfied and all pain will cease.

My hair is still straight and I don't own a Hawaiian shirt or a sports car.

When we turn to God with nothing left but Jesus, we find that Jesus is enough.

So, when we're reading the Bible, when we're praying, when we're worshiping, when we're fellowshipping, when we're ministering, we must do it honestly! Not with an intent to manipulate people, possessions, and positions to try to get momentary relief from our longings, but with a mindset of clinging to God for the only meaning that there is in life, and waiting for heaven when the longing will be completely fulfilled in Jesus. We must deal with the real issues of life not by hiding behind "happy face" masks, but in sincerity, transparency, and tenacity pursuing God!

However, in the meantime, don't let disappointments keep you from enjoying life's true treasures. We can enjoy relationships with loved ones and friends, beautiful music and good literature, athletic activity, helping others, lovely scenery, the color of flowers, watching kittens play, bass fishing, woodworking, and a thousand other things.

These things do not completely or permanently remove the deep longings and pain that provide so much basic motivation in life, but God has given us these things to enjoy. Allow yourself to be driven to God by the longings in your heart. What He wants more than anything from you is a relationship with you and your fellowship. He wants to demonstrate to you that He is the only One who can satisfy.

He doesn't need your Bible study.

He doesn't need your money.

He doesn't need your prayers.

He wants *you*. We have trouble imagining that.

Conclusion

Imagine that you adopt a physically and emotionally abused child, left alone most of the time. You long for a close relationship with this adorable, pathetic little child, but the child's perception of relationships is so distorted she is incapable of receiving the amount of love and acceptance you want to give her. So she remains distant and aloof, playing with her own broken toys in her own little world, while all along, you want to sit her in your lap, cuddle her, and promise her a vacation at Disney World.

So what do you do? You just *love* her unconditionally and wait for the love to soak in until she is able to perceive it and ultimately return it. That is what God does with us.

It is not that we want too much in life; we want too little. We are far too willing to settle for playing with the paltry gadgets and trinkets of our own little world, rather than to nestle in the encircling arms of our Savior and develop a deep, satisfying relationship with the Creator of the universe, the designer-owner of the whole toy store!

He wants you to bring glory to Him by enjoying Him—forever. And when you can dare to believe this, you will clearly see as an act of great love His taking the tawdry, the tarnished, and the transient from your hand so that He can fill them with Himself.

Speed Bump!

Slow down to be sure you've gotten the main points of this chapter.

Question   **Q1.** What are my responsibilities in spiritual growth?

Answer   **A1.** I must *pursue* mature knowledge, character, and ministry.

Q2. What is our motivation for obedience to God?

A2. Our motivation for obedience to God is our *love* for Him who first loved us.

Q3. What is my goal in spiritual growth?

A3. My goal in spiritual growth is to become progressively more like *Christ*.

Q4. What is the danger in pursuing spiritual growth?

A4. The danger in pursuing spiritual growth is trying to find spiritual satisfaction *our* way instead of God's way.

Fill in the Blank

Question
Answer

Q1. What are my responsibilities in spiritual growth?

A1. I must _____ mature knowledge, character, and ministry.

Q2. What is our motivation for obedience to God?

A2. Our motivation for obedience to God is our _____ for Him who first loved us.

Q3. What is my goal in spiritual growth?

A3. My goal in spiritual growth is to become progressively more like

_____ .

Q4. What is the danger in pursuing spiritual growth?

A4. The danger in pursuing spiritual growth is trying to find spiritual satisfaction _____ way instead of God's way.

For Further Thought and Discussion

1. Of the three levels of obedience to God (fear of punishment, agree with wisdom, love for God), which level do you find motivates you the most? Why?

2. Are you growing as rapidly as you would like to grow spiritually? Is there anything you are doing to slow yourself down? Do you have trouble being patient in waiting for spiritual growth? Is there anything you think you could do to speed it up?

3. What area of spiritual growth do you think is most important for you to experience? Why?

4. What things are you tempted to pursue outside of God to get the deep longings of your heart satisfied? Explain.

What If I Don't Believe?

If I don't believe that spiritual growth is a process that takes time, I may get unnecessarily discouraged with my progress. If I don't believe that I have essential responsibilities in the process, I may not assume those responsibilities and miss out on the spiritual growth I long for. If I don't realize how subtle the temptation is to fill my life with things other than God, I may think I am doing fine in the Christian life because I go to church, read my Bible, pray before meals, etc., but not realize that the ache in my heart is because I am not really living for the Lord, but am living for the things of the world.

For Further Study

1. Scripture

- Matthew 22:37–40
- John 15:10–11
- Romans 12:1–2
- 1 Corinthians 13:4–7
- Philippians 2:12–13

2. Books

Rediscovering Holiness, James I. Packer
Desiring God, John Piper
Loving God, Charles Colson

The Bible is a stream wherein the elephant may swim and the lamb may wade.
■ Anonymous

4

How Does the Bible Help Me Grow Spiritually?

Let me tell you about the last flight of the "Lady Be Good." She was a massive bomber during World War II. She had flown many successful missions, puncturing the enemy air space, dropping her load of destruction, and heading back home.

This last flight was different, however. After she reversed course for the return flight, a powerful tailwind pushed her along much faster than normal. When the instruments told the pilots to land, the men looked at their watches and felt that it was much too soon. They faced a critical decision. If they relied on their instruments, they would come down out of the clouds and prepare to land. If they believed their watches, they would keep flying.

To come down too soon might expose them to enemy anti-aircraft fire. On the other hand, if they overshot the airfield, they would perish in the desert. Life and death was in their own hands. Should they trust their instruments, or should they trust their own judgment?

The men chose to ignore the instruments and stick to their gut-level hunch. They stayed up—and overshot the airfield. Their plane was found much later, out of fuel, crashed in the desert. All crewmen had died.

In this chapter we learn that . . .

1. The Bible enlightens and empowers me to grow spiritually.
2. We need the Bible for meaningful life on earth and for hope for eternal life.
3. Our response to the Bible should be total obedience to it.

The story of the "Lady Be Good" is presented as one of the Moody Science Films, and portrays a microcosm of life. We are all flying on the "Lady Be Good" of life. In deciding where and when to land as our final destination, we must either look within ourselves for the answers or search beyond ourselves. We must either trust our gut-level hunches or look for an instrument panel.

The Bible presents itself as the great, cosmic instrument panel. It tells us where we came from, where we are, and where we are going. It is up to us to decide whether or not we accept the "readings" we get from it. Like those that had to be made on the "Lady Be Good," the choices are serious: safe landings or death in the desert.

What Role Does the Bible Play in Spiritual Growth?

The Bible enlightens and empowers me to grow spiritually.

The Bible is not a philosophy book, though it is philosophical. It is not a scientific treatise, though it is consistent with science. It is not a history book, though it is accurate whenever history is recorded. God gave the Bible to man to reveal how man can know God and grow spiritually. Several key passages indicate the importance of Scripture in spiritual growth. In Hebrews 4:12 we read:

[God's word] is full of living power: it is sharper than the sharpest dagger, cutting swift and deep into our innermost thoughts and desires, exposing us for what we really are (The Living Bible).

The Scripture has an inherent power as the Holy Spirit energizes it in our lives. Reading the Scripture is not like reading Shakespeare. It is a body of absolute truth that God uses to penetrate our thought life to its very core and overhaul our attitudes, values, words, and behavior.

In 2 Timothy 3:16–17, we read of the capacity of Scripture to effect complete change in a person:

All Scripture is inspired by God and profitable for teaching, for reproof, for correction, for training in righteousness, that the person of God may be adequate, equipped for every good work (NASB).

The word of God is profitable for what you need to *know* (profitable for teaching), for what you need to *be* (for reproof, for correction, and training in righteousness), and for what you need to *do* (that the man of God may be adequate, thoroughly equipped for every good work).

The writer of Psalm 119 wrote: "Thy word is a lamp unto our feet and a light unto our path" (v. 105).

The picture here is of walking in darkness and not being able to see. You cannot tell if you are headed in the right direction; you cannot tell if you are going to smack into a tree or a grizzly bear; you cannot tell if your path has been erased by a mudslide or sheared off into an abyss; you cannot tell if you are going to get lost altogether. But if you shine a flashlight on your feet, you remedy the entire situation.

The Word lights our path in general but intensifies the places we are to put our feet.

The same is true with life. We inch along in the dark. We cannot tell if we are headed in the right direction, if we might be in danger of an injurious misstep, if we might be going astray, or if we are lost altogether. If we shine the search-light of Scripture onto the path of our life, it saves us from the perils of darkness.

The psalmist also wrote: "Your word I have hidden in my heart that I might not sin against You" (Psalm 119:11). Hiding the word in our heart contributes mightily to the process of transforming us into the character-image of Jesus, a subject that is also found in Romans 12:1–2:

> I urge you therefore, brethren, by the mercies of God, to present your bodies a living and holy sacrifice, acceptable to God, which is your spiritual service of worship, and do not be conformed to this world, but be transformed by the renewing of your mind, that you may prove what the will of God is, that which is good and acceptable and perfect (NASB).

Hiding the word in our heart changes the way we think. This transformation makes us all living demonstrations that God's will is good and perfect and acceptable.

Why I Need to Know This

I need to know this so that I will rely on the Bible as the central resource for my spiritual growth. I need to open my life to the scrutiny of Scripture, take the instruction and hope that it offers, and strive to be fully obedient to it.

You perhaps have heard the story of the airplane which was flying across the continent and encountered a violent thunderstorm. Lightning struck it, knocking out all its navigation equipment. The captain flipped on the intercom and said, "Ladies and gentlemen, I have bad news and good news. The bad news is that our navigation equipment has been knocked out and we have no idea where we are. The good news is that we have a tremendous tailwind, and we are way ahead of schedule."

Without the Bible, our navigation equipment is knocked out. Many of our natural inclinations take us 180 degrees in the opposite direction from truth. We might be making great time, but we have no idea where we are.

These central passages, then, establish the crucial role the Scriptures play in our spiritual maturation process.

Why Do We Need the Bible?

We need the Bible for meaningful life on earth and for hope for eternal life.

For us to have a proper respect for the Bible and a proper regard for its value and importance in giving life meaning, we must understand what happens when a society has no concept of absolute truth. When one person says something is right, another says that it is wrong, they are on the same authority level—they cancel each other out. When that happens, they have to appeal to a higher authority.

For example, two siblings want the same toy. One says, "I want the blue truck." The other retaliates, "No, I want the blue truck." They are deadlocked. So they holler, "Mom!" They appeal to a higher authority for a decision.

In a second example, when two people are in business together and they disagree, they appeal to a higher authority. One takes the other one to court, and the court decides between them; the higher authority of the court is imposed on the situation.

If two entities are deadlocked in determining right and wrong and there is no higher authority immediately available, the stronger one usually imposes his will on the weaker one. If Mom isn't around, then the bigger kid takes the blue truck away from the smaller kid. When that happens, right and wrong have died. The law of the jungle becomes the law of the land, the survival of the fittest.

In a larger context, if two nations disagree, they go to war. There is no higher authority to which they can appeal.

When it comes to moral issues, the only higher authority you can appeal to is God. If you disagree with someone on a moral issue, you can go to God's word and settle the issue there. However, if both of you do not believe in God, then that eliminates the "higher authority." When that happens, you can no longer talk about right and wrong. You can only talk about preferences. You can say, "I prefer that you not cheat on your income tax," but you cannot say, "It is wrong to cheat on your income tax." If you say **God is the highest moral arbiter.** it is wrong to cheat on your income tax and someone else says it is not wrong, and if you have no higher authority to determine the rightness or wrongness, then you cancel each other out.

Do you feel it is wrong for a person to come into your home, rob you, violate your wife and daughter, kill you, and then burn your house down to conceal the evidence? All that sounds wrong. But if you do not appeal to a higher authority, then you have no basis upon which to call those acts wrong, even though you may be violently opposed to them personally. You might say, "This is wrong." But the criminal says, "No, it isn't. For me, it is right." So the criminal imposes his view on you with no consideration for absolute truth.

An excellent historical case in point is the extermination of the Jews by Hitler. If absolute truth does not exist, then by what authority does anyone say what Hitler did is wrong? You say it was wrong, but Hitler says it was right. You are two human beings. You cancel each other out.

The same thing holds true with less heinous examples, but which still have a major destructive impact on society. Take, for example, white collar crime on Wall Street, or selling drugs, or padding defense contracts and bilking the government out of millions of dollars, or adultery and marital infidelity; if there is no absolute truth, then the only wrong is getting caught.

Now do you glimpse the magnitude of the importance of the Bible for society? With a respect for biblical truth, you can build relationships and a society in which the innocent are protected. Without it, you cannot.

In an editorial in his newsletter, *Jubilee,* Chuck Colson wrote:

> I have argued that we are living in an age advancing backwards. Where once stood a standard of truth and authority is now a fearsome freedom and autonomy. Modern men and women, having elevated the individual above all else, hold no principles except their passions to plot their paths—nothing above themselves to respect or obey, nothing to live or die for.

And, as I've argued, such egoism destroys individual character, in turn undermining the very institutions upon which our society depends.

Our crisis, at root, is one of individual character. Therefore, our principle task must be to reawaken those internal restraints on passion and self-interest that are the very substance of character. Our task is moral education.

But there can be no moral education without moral absolutes. The term *moral* is obsolete unless we can appeal to God for His absolutes.

Second, regarding hope for eternal life, we have no knowledge of or hope for eternal life outside the Bible. Only in the Scripture do we learn that our sin has separated us from God, and that only through Jesus can we be reconciled to God and have the hope of eternal life in heaven.

How Should We Respond to the Bible?

Our response to the Bible should be total obedience to it.

Two tasks of obedience delineate the road to happiness: the elimination of the negatives and the introduction of the positives. We must eradicate those glaring sins of commission—lying, cheating, stealing, immorality, drunkenness. But that only puts us half way to experiencing the abundant life which God envisions for us. The other half involves the introduction of the positives—that is, consistently loving God and others, even in the small things.

For example, it is one thing to stop beating your wife; it is another to love her as Christ loved the church and gave Himself up for her. It is one thing to stop yelling at your child; it is another to bring him up in the nurture and instruction of the Lord. It is one thing to stop swearing; it is another to "let no unwholesome word proceed from your mouth, but only such a word as is good for edification according to the need of the moment, that it may give grace to those who hear" (Ephesians 4:29, NASB).

It is not until we have put off the things we ought not do and put on the things we ought to do that we have responded fully to the Bible.

Conclusion

All of God's truth is absolute truth. It is all intended by God to be followed. Consequences follow when it is not. As Christians, our response to absolute truth is to be total. We will fail, but we will be better off for trying and failing than if we never tried at all.

The Bible is God's owner's manual for humanity. He knows how humanity works. He knows what will work well for us and what will harm us. If we operate according to the instruction manual, our machinery will run well. If we disregard the manual, things big and little break down. This applies to new Christians as well as mature Christians. Each of us has areas in which God is working in us, and we must respond as best we can to the truth as we understand it. We must take the Bible seriously, from beginning to end!

In an old episode of the comic strip *B.C.*, the cave man is leaning over the ever-present boulder, and on the rock is inscribed "Trivia Test." B.C. is administering the exam to one of his prehistoric buddies. "Here's one from the Bible," he says. "What were the last words uttered by Lot's wife?" His furry friend replies: "Phooey on your fanatical beliefs. I'm going to take one last look."

In many ways, we are tempted to imitate the behavior of Lot's wife. But just as she lost, so would we. We'd best take the Bible seriously.

Speed Bump!

Slow down to be sure you've gotten the main points from this chapter.

Question   **Q1.**   What role does the Bible play in spiritual growth?

Answer   **A1.**   The Bible *enlightens* and *empowers* me to grow spiritually.

Q2.   Why do we need the Bible?

A2.   We need the Bible for *meaningful* life on earth and for hope for *eternal* life.

Q3. How should we respond to the Bible?

A3. Our response to the Bible should be *total obedience* to it.

Fill in the Blank

Question   **Q1.**   What role does the Bible play in spiritual growth?

Answer   **A1.**   The Bible _____ and _____ me to grow spiritually.

Q2. Why do we need the Bible?

A2. We need the Bible for _____ life on earth and for hope for _____ life.

Q3. How should we respond to the Bible?

A3. Our response to the Bible should be _____ _____ to it.

For Further Thought and Discussion

1. What do you think holds most people back from studying the Bible more faithfully? How do you think that barrier could be overcome?

2. What problems in our society today do you believe can be traced directly to a rejection of Scripture?

3. Why do you think more people are not more obedient to what the Bible teaches? What do you think could be done to overcome that barrier?

What If I Don't Believe?

If I don't believe the Bible is essential to my spiritual growth, I will not be motivated to learn the Bible well. I may be content to limit my biblical knowledge to what I hear in church on Sunday mornings. If I don't believe the truth of Scripture is essential to meaningful life on earth and eternal life in heaven, I may be tempted to be careless in my obedience to it.

For Further Study

1. Scripture

- Psalm 119:105, 111
- Romans 12:1–3
- 2 Timothy 3:16–17
- Hebrews 4:12

2. Books

Living by the Book, Howard Hendricks
How to Study Your Bible, Kay Arthur

*We are born helpless. As soon as we are fully
conscious we discover loneliness. We need others
physically, emotionally, intellectually. We need them if
we are to know anything, even ourselves.*
■ C. S. Lewis

5

How Do Other Believers Help
Me Grow Spiritually?

The seagull, on the surface, is a beautiful bird—a dazzling white feathered kite sailing serenely against a brilliant blue background. Since the early seventies, with the publication of a runaway best-selling book, *Jonathan Livingston Seagull*, the seagull has been immortalized as a symbol of freedom, grace, and beauty. Beneath the surface, however, the seagull does not live up to its initial impression. In reality, it is a nasty, dirty little bird. Seagulls scavenge on garbage and refuse. They will eat the unprotected young of other seagulls. They are loners that will attack another gull that gets too close to them. If a white gull happens to rub up against a bright color of wet paint and becomes different in marking from the rest of the birds, the other birds may attack it and kill it. Beneath the surface of their dazzling exterior, they are aggressive, selfish, dirty, nasty, disgusting little birds.

Canadian geese contrast sharply with the seagulls. On the surface, they are not beautiful birds. They are short, squat, dumpy, brown, black and gray waddlers. But up close, the Canadian geese are remarkable birds. They mate for life. They are devoted to their young, never leaving them exposed to danger. Both parents care for their offspring, sharing the nesting duties and trading off on the responsibilities of feeding and guarding the goslings.

All the geese look out for each other. In fact, some mothers will baby-sit for geese of another family. The flock will not migrate until the young are strong enough to fly. If a very young goose or an older goose is unable to maintain the pace of the main flock and needs more rest, other geese will stay with them until they are strong enough to make the flight. As they travel, they fly in a "V" formation, with the lead bird breaking the air, making it easier for the others to

In this chapter we learn that . . .

1. I need other believers because God has created me to live in mutual dependence and fellowship with them.
2. My responsibility to other Christians is to love them and serve them with my spiritual gift.
3. My responsibility to receive from other Christians is to allow them to love me and minister their gift to me.

fly; and they trade off lead positions so that no one goose gets too tired. Though they are not white, streamlined, and beautiful, behavior-wise the Canadian geese are marvelous, admirable birds.

As Christians we need to ask ourselves, if we were birds, what kind of bird would we be? Would we be a seagull or a Canadian goose? In the great Audubon Society of life, God calls upon us to be not seagulls, but Canadian geese.

Why Do I Need Other Believers?

I need other believers because God has created me to live in mutual dependence and fellowship with them.

The universal church is a spiritual entity made up of all Christians, past, present, and future. The local church, however, is a specific, local congregation of Christians who have agreed to band together to pursue the goals and responsibilities of the universal church. From the earliest days of Christianity, the confessions of faith have stated that we are "one, holy, catholic (universal), apostolic church." This is the body of Christ in the world, intended to function as Christ would if He were still on earth.

But only by belonging to a visible community of faith (local church) can an individual truly make manifest the spiritual reality of the universal church. And only by belonging to a local church can individual Christians fulfill the commands of Christ.

From the very beginning, God planned that the universal church would be manifested by "confessing communities" (local congregations) to fulfill His mission on earth—to worship God, to build up believers, to impact the world through evangelism and humanitarianism, to preach the word, to administer the sacraments, and to administer church discipline. Immediately after Pentecost (the day the New Testament church was born—

Acts 2), God established the pattern: individual believers were to gather together into local communities.

Why I Need to Know This

I need to know this so that I will integrate myself into the lives of other Christians, learn from them, imitate their lifestyles, fellowship with them, help them, and let them help me. I need to know that God has created me to need other Christians, and that I cannot be the Christian God wants me to be unless I embrace the corporate nature of being Christian. Otherwise, I might believe that I can make it as a spiritual Lone Ranger. I might be deceived into thinking that I don't need other Christians, that I don't need church, that I don't need to do anything for others or let others do anything for me.

I used to pastor a church in the most independent nation in the world (United States), in the most independent state in the nation (Texas), in the most independent city in Texas (Austin), and perhaps the most independent church in Austin. If it never had been before, it became abundantly clear then that we Americans like our independence. We don't like anyone telling us what to do—how to raise our children, who to vote for, or whether to join a church.

A widespread belief today in the United States postulates that a person can be a Christian apart from the church. Now certainly a person can be saved apart from a local church, but a person cannot fulfill his spiritual destiny apart from a local church. Two pictures of the New Testament church describe (1) a building in which individuals are the stones that make up the building, and (2) a body in which the members make up the different physical parts. In the eyes of God, a Christian is no more normal functioning alone than a brick lying apart from the building or a hand severed from the rest of the body.

In the Book of Acts, each believer who made a profession of faith and was baptized became part of a local congregation. For

A person cannot fulfill his spiritual destiny apart from a local church.

the first Christians in the Bible, membership in a local church seemed little more optional than membership in the universal church. Unfortunately, membership in a local church has fallen into disfavor in recent decades. Strong commitment to local churches seems at an all time low. This is wrong. Martin Luther, the father of the Reformation, said, "Apart from the church, salvation is impossible." We might think that is a little strong, but if we take the example and teaching of the Bible, we would have to agree that membership in a local church should be a mark of salvation.

Calvin, another Reformation hero, wrote,

> So highly does the Lord esteem the communion of His church that He considers everyone a traitor and apostate from religion who perversely withdraws himself from any Christian society which preserves the true ministry of the word and sacraments (*Institutes*, 2:1012).

This, too, might seem overstated. However, we cannot ignore the truth in it. We cannot join together in corporate worship of God apart from the local church. The gifted members of the universal church cannot build up one another to maturity in Christ outside of the local church. Impacting the world through evangelism and humanitarianism cannot be effected outside the local church. The witness to the deity of Christ cannot be proclaimed and the validity of the gospel cannot be asserted without unity among Christians in local communities.

Outside of belonging to a local congregation, Christians have no sense of history and continuity, no perception of belonging to something greater than themselves, and no feeling of accountability for godly behavior.

Seen biblically, a first step of discipleship (following Christ) is membership in a local church. The responsibility of those who are involved with new converts is to guide them, not just into individual prayer and Bible study, but also into a local church where the Word is taught, the ordinances of baptism and the Lord's Supper are observed, church discipline is taken seriously, and fellowship and mutual ministry to one another are practiced. The local church and the universal church are to support each other.

We must abandon the thought that we are self-sufficient.

God does not want us to be able to make it alone. In fact, He has stacked the deck against us so that we *cannot* make it alone. We must have others. He does not want us to be seagulls, but Canadian geese. He does not want us to be the Lone Ranger, but the Three Musketeers. He does not want us to be an island or a rock, but a bridge and an oasis. I need you, and you need me! God has seen to it. We must dispel the notion that we can make it alone. We must abandon the thought that we are self-sufficient.

We must relinquish the impression that we do not need others. We *need* others and others *need* us.

Let's look at the biblical evidence for this. In Ephesians 4:11–13, 15–16, we read:

> [Christ] gave some to be apostles, some to be prophets, some to be evangelists, and some to be pastors and teachers, to prepare God's people for works of service, so that the body of Christ may be built up until we all reach unity in the faith and in the knowledge of the Son of God and become mature, attaining to the whole measure of the fullness of Christ. . . . Speaking the truth in love, we will in all things grow up into him who is the Head, that is, Christ. From him the whole body, joined and held together by every supporting ligament, grows and builds itself up in love, as each part does its work (NIV).

The body of Christ is built up as each person contributes to the welfare of the whole. The more people contributing, the healthier the body. The fewer people participating, the less healthy the body.

In his remarkable book *Fearfully and Wonderfully Made*, Dr. Paul Brand has written:

> Chemically, [the cells in my body] are almost alike, but visually, and functionally they are as different as the animals in a zoo. Red blood cells, discs resembling Lifesaver candies, voyage through my blood loaded with oxygen to feed the other cells. Muscle cells, which absorb so much of that nourishment, are sleek and supple, full of coiled energy. Cartilage cells with shiny black nuclei look like bunches of black-eyed peas glued tightly together for strength. Fat cells seem lazy and leaden, like bulging white plastic garbage bags jammed together.
>
> Bone cells live in rigid structures that exude strength. The aristocrats of the cellular world are the nerve cells.
>
> I believe these cells in my body can teach me about larger organisms: families, groups, communities, villages, nations—and especially about one specific community of people that is likened to a body more than thirty times in the New Testament. I speak of the Body of Christ, that network of people scattered across the planet who have little in common other than their membership in a group that follows Jesus Christ.
>
> My body employs a bewildering zoo of cells, none of which individually resembles the larger body. Just so, Christ's Body comprises an unlikely assortment of humans (27)

That's the body—a host of individuals, vastly different from each other but each playing an important part in giving life and purpose to the whole.

In another passage dealing with the interrelatedness of Christians, we read:

> Let us consider how we may spur one another on toward love and good deeds. Let us not give up meeting together, as some are in the habit of doing, but let us encourage one another (Hebrews 10:23–25).

We are to get together regularly to help one another live godly lives, and this mutual encouragement is not optional—it is essential. If we are to grow to maturity in Christ, we must have the ministry of mutual encouragement. The Bible is filled with references to "one another."

- Romans 12:5—We are members of one another.

- Romans 12:10—be devoted to one another in brotherly love.

- Romans 12:10—honor one another above yourselves.

- Romans 15:5—be of the same mind with one another.

- Romans 15:7—accept one another.

- Romans 15:14—admonish one another.

- Romans 16:16—greet one another.

- Galatians 5:13—serve one another in love.

- Galatians 6:2—bear one another's burdens.

- Ephesians 4:2—bearing with one another in love.

- Ephesians 5:21—submit to one another out of reverence for Christ.

- 1 Thessalonians 5:11—encourage one another and build each other up.

Scripture emphasizes our need for each other in order for us to prosper spiritually. To even imagine that we can be robust Christians apart from a vital relationship in a healthy local church is fallacy.

It is easy to see why we have gotten confused on this issue. For one reason, some churches and even denominations have abused their authority over their members and no longer deserve to be followed. Another reason is that a given local church on a given Sunday morning may have in attendance more hypocrites, more agnostics, more cultural Christians there just for the show, and more unbelievers than they do committed and sincere followers of Christ. It is easy to get cynical when we see this.

But none of this changes the Bible. Committed Christians are to find other committed Christians to join together to follow the ideals and commands of the universal church.

Our response to this, then, is twofold. First, we must give of ourselves to others, and second, we must be willing to receive from others when appropriate. No one can give something unless someone else is willing to receive it.

What Is My Responsibility to Give to Other Christians?

My responsibility to other Christians is to love them and serve them with my spiritual gift.

Our first responsibility to other Christians is to love them. Galatians 6:10 says, "Therefore, as we have opportunity, let us do good to all, especially to those who are of the household of faith."

The "good" that we are to do may take many forms. Perhaps someone needs money or some type of physical help, and we have the ability to help them (James 2:16). The good that we might do might be acts of kindness. The apostle Paul wrote in Ephesians 4:32, "Be kind to one another, tender-hearted, forgiving one another, even as God in Christ also forgave you." Or it may be as simple as an encouraging word. In his book entitled *Encouragement*, Larry Crabb tells this story:

> As a young person, I developed the humiliating problem of stuttering. I was elected president of my class in the ninth grade, and was called upon in a large assembly to be inducted during a ceremony. The principal said, "I, Larry Crabb, of Plymouth-Whitemarsh Junior High School, do hereby promise . . . etc." I said, "I L-L-L-L-Larry Crabb, of P-P-P-Plymouth-Whitemarsh Junior High School, do hereby p-p-p-p-promise . . . etc."

The principal was sympathetically perplexed, my favorite English teacher wanted to cry, a few students laughed out loud, most were awkwardly amused, some felt bad for me—and I died a thousand deaths.

A short time later, I was called upon to pray during communion. Filled less with worship than stark terror, I became confused to the point of heresy. I remember thanking the Father for hanging on the cross, and praising Christ for triumphantly bringing the spirit from the grave. Stuttering throughout, I finally thought of the word "amen," (perhaps the first evidence of the Spirit's leading), said it, and sat down. I recall staring at the floor, too embarrassed to look around.

When the service was over, I darted for the door, hoping to escape before someone came to correct my twisted theology. I was too late. Jim Dunbar intercepted me. I recoiled as he put his arm around me. "Just endure this, and then get to the car," I said to myself. I then listened to this godly gentleman speak words that I can repeat verbatim today, more than twenty years later.

"Larry," he said, "there's one thing I want you to know. Whatever you do for the Lord, I'm behind you one thousand percent." Then he walked away.

Even as I write these words, my eyes fill with tears. Those words were life words. They had power. They reached deep into my being. They encouraged me! (24)

> **Everyone is gifted to do something, and the church needs everyone desperately.**

Not only must we give to others general acts and words of kindness and generosity, but we must also share with them our spiritual gifts. First Peter 4:10 says, "As each one has received a gift, minister it to one another, as good stewards of the manifold grace of God."

Each of us has a gift, and even if it is not an easily recognized gift, it is our gift, given by God for the good of others. We must use it. For example, when someone stands before a group and preaches, teaches, disciples, or counsels, their contribution to the body of Christ is obvious. But these people are a minority. What about the majority of people who are not gifted in this way? We have allowed an elitist mentality to sneak into our churches if those who cannot preach, teach, disciple, or counsel think they can't do anything.

This type of thinking unfortunately affects the whole church. First, it keeps those who are not gifted in those ways from understanding their importance to the body of Christ and creates a feeling of inferiority. Just as bad, the body of Christ does not benefit from their ministry. Both the individual and the church suffer.

Everyone is gifted to do something, and we need everyone desperately. Take, for example, the people necessary to conduct a normal weekly church service—those who:

- show love and tenderness to the tots in the church nursery each Sunday morning,

- teach the children and make them feel important and wanted in the Sunday school classes,

- unlock the doors on Sunday morning and lock them up again on Sunday afternoon,

- come to church on Saturday evening to make sure the heat or air conditioning is on and that everything is working,

- cut the grass so the facility is attractive,

- stuff the bulletins and put mailing labels on the newsletter,

- baby-sit the children so that the mothers of preschoolers can have a free morning of encouragement and fellowship,

- come early to set up a classroom,

- prepare communion elements,

- help in Vacation Bible School and children's musicals,

- look out for visitors each Sunday to make them feel welcome,

- fix meals for families of new mothers,

- provide roses on the pulpit,

- take flowers to those in the hospital,

- write to the missionaries,

- open homes for youth parties,

- provide transportation for youth events,

- organize sports teams and events,

- operate the tape ministry,

- and the scores of others who did not get mentioned—all these are heroes!

Of course, this says nothing of all who have ministries outside the church. We must all realize that we serve God by serving people. If all of us stopped doing our ministry Saturday night, the church would shut down Sunday morning. It is true that most *do not get* the recognition they deserve. Nevertheless, many people know and appreciate their unsung labor. And God knows and appreciates. Their reward in heaven will be just as great as a Billy Graham's because God rewards faithfulness.

What Is My Responsibility to Receive From Other Christians?

My responsibility to receive from other Christians is to allow them to love me and serve me with their gift.

We began this discussion by saying that there were two ways for us to respond to the reality that Christians need each other. First, we must be willing to give of our selves to the needs of others. Second, we must be willing to receive from others when appropriate.

When you have a physical need and someone offers to help, accept it. They are offering because they care. They are doing what they have been gifted and prompted by God to do. If you are a new mother and someone brings you meals for a few days, accept them. If you are in financial need and someone slips you a nice check, accept it. If you are in need of counsel and someone whispers words of wisdom, accept them. Unless there is an overriding reason not to accept the proffered gift, receive it. Things are supposed to work that way.

As to your spiritual growth, if someone is offering something you need, accept it. If it is Bible knowledge, discipleship, or training and you don't know where to get what you need, start asking and looking around. Somewhere someone gifted can help fill your spiritual lack.

As to encouragement, if someone says something nice to you, don't deny it. Don't deprecate yourself, run yourself down, or invent a story showing that you don't deserve the encouragement. Accept it. Say "Thank you." In order for the body to work as it is intended to work, we must be willing to give, and we must be willing to receive.

Conclusion

John Donne, early in the sixteen hundreds, captured the spirit of the unity of the body of Christ when he wrote:

No man is an island, entire of itself; every man is a piece of the continent, a part of the main; if a clod be washed away by the sea, Europe is the less, as well as if a promontory were, as well as if a manor of thy friends or of thine own were; any man's death diminishes me, because I am involved in mankind; and therefore never send to know for whom the bell tolls; it tolls for thee. (*Devotions upon Emergent Occasions*, No. 17)

We in the body of Christ are part of one another. We are not entire of ourselves. We were made by God to love and be loved, to give and receive ministry. The Bible mandates this. We must give to others our spiritual gifts, our resources, our encouragement. And we must be willing to receive the same from others. We must be willing to live together in mutual ministry and love.

Speed Bump!
Slow down to be sure you've gotten the main points of this chapter.

Question
Answer

Q1. Why do I need other believers?

A1. I need other believers because God has created me to live in *mutual* dependence and fellowship with them.

Q2. What is my responsibility to give to other Christians?

A2. My responsibility to other Christians is to *love* them and *serve* them with my spiritual gift.

Q3. What is my responsibility to receive from other Christians?

A3. My responsibility to receive from other Christians is to allow them to *love* me and *serve* me with their gift.

Fill in the Blank

Question
Answer

Q1. Why do I need other believers?

A1. I need other believers because God has created me to live in _____ dependence and fellowship with them.

Q2. What is my responsibility to give to other Christians?

A2. My responsibility to other Christians is to _____ them and _____ them with my spiritual gift.

Q3. What is my responsibility to receive from other Christians?

A3. My responsibility to receive from other Christians is to allow them to _____ me and _____ me with their gift.

For Further Thought and Discussion

1. Do you really believe that God has created you to live in mutual dependence and fellowship with other believers? What if you don't like church? What if you don't like the Christians you know? What if you don't feel like living mutual fellowship and dependence with others? What should you do?

2. It is easy to love people you know and like. But can you love people if you don't like them or don't know them? What do you think is the most valuable thing you can do for others? Do you think that might be your spiritual gift?

3. Do you find it easier to give to others, or to allow others to give to you? Many people fall into one of two extremes. Either they will not let anyone help them, or else they sponge off other people. Which extreme do you tend to lean toward? What do you think is the proper balance in allowing others to help you?

What If I Don't Believe?

If I don't believe the church is important, I may try to live the Christian life without the fellowship and support of other Christians, and I may not understand why my Christian life doesn't seem to be working as well as it should. Also, I will not have the satisfaction of being able to live my life for something bigger than myself. In addition, acute needs in my life will go unmet because I will not get close enough to others to allow them to help me.

For Further Study

1. Scripture

- Galatians 6:10
- Ephesians 4:11–16
- Hebrews 10:23–25
- James 2:16
- 1 Peter 4:10

2. Books

The Body, Charles Colson
The Purpose Driven Church, Rick Warren
Building Up One Another, Gene Getz

We are always on the forge, or on the anvil; by trials
God is shaping us for higher things.
■ Henry Ward Beecher (1813–1887)

How Do Time and Trials Help Me Grow Spiritually?

Every fall the monarch caterpillar crawls to the end of a twig, fashions a meticulously fabricated cocoon around itself, slams the door, and goes to sleep. Some time later, something utterly miraculous happens. Out crawls a butterfly! Somehow, by some power hidden deep in the mysteries of nature, a fat, low-slung, many-legged, ugly little creature of the earth is changed into a light, sleek, brightly-colored, beautiful little creature of the sky. How it happens, or even that it happens, is one of the true glories of nature.

As we probe into this mystery, however, we learn some startling truths. If you walked past the low tree limb where the cocoon was attached at just the precise moment the butterfly began to emerge from its magic chamber, you would see a fearful struggle—a struggle that would rend your heart and make you fear for the butterfly's life. The butterfly pushes and pulls and wiggles. Then it falls back, exhausted. It repeats the process again and again until, finally, after long and agonizing labor, it escapes the cocoon.

In this chapter we learn that . . .

1. The Bible teaches that spiritual growth requires time, just as physical growth does.
2. The Bible teaches that trials are used by God to make us spiritually insightful and strong.
3. The Bible gives us many examples of spiritual leaders whose trials eventually produced spiritual maturity.

As you watched this struggle for life—as indeed it is, for if the butterfly does not get out within a certain length of time, it will die in the cocoon—you would be tempted to come to the butterfly's rescue, perhaps by taking some tweezers and enlarging the opening ever so slightly to let the butterfly out of his potential coffin.

Well-meaning as such a gesture would be, it would seal the doom of the butterfly. For the very struggle to get out of the cocoon develops the butterfly's ability to fly. If the butterfly does not struggle to get out of the cocoon, it is condemned to crawl the twigs, unable to fly, until it starves to death or becomes dinner for a waiting bird.

Both time in the cocoon and the trials in getting out of it are essential to transform the ugly little caterpillar into a beautiful flitting butterfly. Time and trials are both necessary to transform a worm-like creature, condemned to inching its way along the underbrush of life, into a lovely winged creature able to take to the heavens.

The natural realm with butterflies parallels the spiritual realm with children of God. God wants us to undergo continuous transformation from creatures of the physical realm to creatures of the spiritual realm, from creatures of the world to creatures of heaven, from creatures of time to creatures of eternity. With our bodies on earth, God wants us to live with our minds on heaven.

And just as it takes time and trials to transform a caterpillar into a butterfly, so it takes time and trials to transform a child of God from one whose interests, values, and affections center on earth to one whose interests, values, and affections focus on heaven.

What Does the Bible Teach About the Role of Time in Spiritual Growth?

The Bible teaches that spiritual growth requires time, just as physical growth does.

In 1 Peter 2:2, the apostle instructs us "as newborn babes, desire the pure milk of the word, that you may grow thereby." This relates physical growth to spiritual growth. We grow slowly physically—and spiritually. When I was twelve to fourteen years old, I drove my saintly mother nuts jumping. I had inherited a jumping gene from somewhere, and I loved to jump. I jumped until I could touch the eight-foot ceiling. Then I jumped until I could hit my hand flat against it. Then I jumped until I could hit it with my elbow. Then I jumped until I could hit it with my head.

All of this was done with a corresponding love for and devotion to basketball, where jumping was a valuable ability. But no matter how tall I was or how high I could jump, I always wanted to be taller and to jump higher.

The same was true spiritually when I became a Christian after my first year in college. As I look back on it, I experienced rather significant spiritual growth from the very beginning. But it never seemed enough. I was never pleased with how far I had come. I was always consumed with how far it seemed I had to go.

But any growth takes time, and while it is always appropriate to do the things that encourage maximum growth, we must be content with our present stature, physical or spiritual, or life will be troubling indeed.

Why I Need to Know This

Unless I realize that spiritual growth requires time, I may think that my slow pace of spiritual growth is due to something inherently deficient in me. Unless I understand that God often uses trials to make me stronger, I may conclude that God is punishing me or is angry with me for some reason I don't understand.

In Luke 2:52, we read that Jesus kept increasing in wisdom and stature, and in favor with God and men. He waited until He was thirty years old to minister. *Growth over time.*

In a similar vein we read in Romans 12:1–2, "Do not be conformed to this world, but be transformed by the renewing of your mind." *Growth over time.*

In 1 Corinthians 3:6 Paul writes, "I planted, Apollos watered, but God gave the increase." *Growth over time.*

One of the qualifications for an elder, a spiritual leader in the church, is that he not be a new convert (1 Timothy 3:6). *Growth over time.*

You cannot become holy in a hurry!

What Does the Bible Teach About the Role of Trials in Spiritual Growth?

The Bible teaches that trials are used by God to make us spiritually insightful and strong.

One teaching afoot says if you are in God's will, you will not have trials. You will not have physical ailments, or financial difficulties, or relationship problems. It teaches that if you have enough faith, God will heal you of those things. It says that if you claim what you want as though it were already true, it will become true.

However, some of the fundamental passages in Scripture disclaim this teaching. In Psalm 119:67, 71, and 75 we read:

> Before I was afflicted I went astray,
> But now I keep Thy word.
> It is good for me that I was afflicted,
> That I may learn Thy statutes.
> I know, O Lord, that Thy judgments are righteous,
> And that in faithfulness Thou hast afflicted me (NASB).

This passage teaches very clearly that the Lord afflicted David for the purpose of maturing him. We see also in 2 Corinthians 4:8–11 and 16–18 that Paul suffered tremendously:

> We are afflicted in every way, but not crushed; perplexed, but not despairing; persecuted, but not forsaken; struck down, but not destroyed; always carrying about in the body the dying of Jesus, that the life of Jesus also may be manifested in our body. For we who live are constantly being delivered over to death for Jesus' sake, that the life of Jesus also may be manifested in our mortal flesh. . . . Therefore we do not lose heart, but though our outer man is decaying, yet our inner man is being renewed day by day. For momentary, light affliction is producing for us an eternal weight of glory far beyond all comparison, while we look not at the things which are seen, but at the things which are not seen; for the things which are seen are temporal, but the things which are not seen are eternal (NASB).

Again, in James 1:2–4 we see:

> Consider it all joy, my brethren, when [not if] you encounter various trials, knowing that the testing of your faith produces endurance. And let endurance have its perfect result, that you may be perfect and complete, lacking in nothing (NASB).

Trials produce endurance, endurance produces maturity.

Finally, we see in 1 Peter 2:18–21:

> Servants, be submissive to your masters with all respect, not only to those who are good and gentle, but also to those who are unreasonable. For this finds favor, if for the sake of conscience toward God a man bears up under sorrows when suffering unjustly. For what

credit is there if, when you sin and are harshly treated, you endure it with patience? But if when you do what is right and suffer for it you patiently endure it, this finds favor with God. For you have been called for this purpose, since Christ also suffered for you, leaving you an example for you to follow in His steps (NASB).

God's will includes suffering, and Christ left us an example by His own suffering. Verse 17 says that we may suffer for doing right.

You cannot become holy in a hurry.

Christ suffered, we read in 1 Peter 4:1, and we should arm ourselves for the same purpose. Chapter 4:12–16 indicates that we can glorify God in our suffering, and finally in 5:10–11 we see that our suffering can result in strength and maturity.

We must dispel the notion that the Christian life does not include suffering. Otherwise, it will distort our perspective, confuse us, frustrate us, and cause us to think something is wrong with us.

Not only does the will of God include trials, it includes trials over time—you cannot have one bad day, and wake up the next day spiritually mature.

Someone once asked the president of his school whether he could not take a shorter course than the one prescribed. "Oh yes," replied the president, "but then, it depends upon what you want to be. When God wants to make an oak, He takes a hundred years, but when He wants to make a squash, He takes six months."

If you want to be a spiritual squash, you can make it in a hurry. But if you want to be an oak, you must sink your roots deep and dig in for the long haul.

What Examples Does the Bible Give Us of the Role of Time and Trials?

The Bible gives us many examples of spiritual leaders whose trials eventually produced spiritual maturity.

Perhaps the most vivid and heartening way to grasp this truth is to see it fleshed out in the lives of some of the giants of the Scripture. For example, God gave Joseph reason to believe that God was going to use him in an extraordinary way. Yet each time Joseph tried to do something right, circumstances backfired on him and he paid dearly for it.

He tried to get his brothers to shape up by telling them about the dreams he had. But the dreams indicated God was going to cause Joseph to rule over them. They didn't like that, and Joseph paid for it by their selling him as a slave.

He tried to do the right thing by resisting the advances of Potiphar's wife. She retaliated by having him imprisoned. He tried to do the right thing in prison, but the man he befriended forgot about him, and Joseph languished in prison for another two years. Finally, God plucked him out of the prison and set him over the entire nation of Egypt.

In a second example, David was anointed by Samuel to be king over Israel fourteen years before he came to the throne. During that time, rather than living like a prince, David was running from cave to cave like a common criminal, trying to keep Saul from lopping off his head.

In the New Testament, Jesus told Paul that He was going to use Paul to take the message of salvation to the Gentile world. Fourteen years later Paul set out on his first missionary journey. During that time, Paul sewed tents, lived in the desert, and endured unsatisfying experiences with Jewish Christians in Jerusalem.

Spiritual growth takes not only time but trials. Between the time that God gave Joseph and David and Paul those promises and the time He fulfilled them was at least ten years, and easily more. During that time, God put them through the types of experiences that developed in them the strength of character, the sense of right and wrong, the compassion for others, and the vision for the future that they would need as leaders.

What was true of the spiritual giants of the Bible must be equally true for us: growth takes time and it takes trials. We cannot become holy quickly or easily.

Our response to these realities, then, must be to cultivate patience. Patience isn't one of the stronger virtues for most of us. I'm afraid my ultimate character was revealed at the age of four or five when someone told me that a peach pit was a seed, and that if I planted it, it would grow into a peach tree. So I ran out to the sand box in the back yard and planted the peach pit. I waited anxiously until the next morning when I raced out to see my peach tree. But no peach tree had sprouted. In a fit of anger, which I remember clearly to this day, I ripped the peach pit out of the sand and threw it as far into the adjoining field as my chubby little fingers could throw it. I have been struggling for patience ever since.

The writer to Hebrews says that we must run with patience (endurance) the race that is set before us (12:1).

In addition to patience, we must persevere. Passive patience is not what is called for. Active patience fits the need. We *will* fail. And when we do, we must get back up and try again. The person is not a failure who falls down, but who refuses to get up. How many times? Seven times seventy or as many times as it happens—that is how many times God will forgive you, so that is how many times you must forgive yourself.

No one enjoys failure, but God can make failure the back door to success. He did for Joseph, for David, for Paul—and He can for us.

Conclusion

Amy Carmichael was an English missionary to India in the first half of the twentieth century. She had a particular burden for children who were confiscated to use as temple prostitutes by the Hindu priests. An accident in 1931 left her an invalid, crippled with arthritis. She remained mostly bedridden for nearly twenty years.

From a human perspective, that is so hard to understand. How, why would God allow such a brilliant, talented, dedicated servant of His to become so crippled that she could no longer serve Him as she once did, and live out her life in pain and misery? Yet Amy Carmichael met her pain with God-given grace and made a wonderful impact on the world for the cause of Christ even from her bed of pain. She wrote many stories which have touched hundreds of thousands of lives. She let her adversity make her spiritually stronger.

Like Job, who lost all that he had yet did not curse God; like Paul who in spite of persistent prayer for relief lived with a "thorn in the flesh"; like many other of God's choice servants, Amy Carmichael submitted to the pain and suffering—and as a result was blessed and used greatly by God.

Out of her own furnace of trials, Amy Carmichael wrote a deep and moving poem about pain entitled, "No Scar?"

> Hast Thou no scar?
> No hidden scar on foot, or side, or hand?
> I hear thee sung as mighty in the land,
> I hear them hail thy bright ascendant star,
> Hast thou no scar?
>
> Has thou no wound?
> Yet I was wounded by the archers, spent,
> Leaned Me against a tree to die; and rent
> By ravening beasts that compassed Me, I swooned:
> Has thou no wound?
>
> No wound? No scar?
> Yet, as the Master shall the servant be,
> And pierced are the feet that follow Me;
> But thine are whole: can he have followed far
> Who has nor wound nor scar?
> (Amy Carmichael, *Toward Jerusalem*, quoted by Russell
> Hitt in *How Christians Grow* 66)

We may shrink at the prospect of having to be wounded in order to mature. But we may all find grace and resolve in the words of Job, who suffered so greatly as a testimony to the grace of God: "When He has tested me, I shall come forth as gold" (Job 23:10). Gold, mined from the ground, is often imbedded in dirt, rocks, iron ore, and mineral deposits. The refiner puts the mixed-up mess into a cauldron, where it melts under near white-hot heat. Since gold is so heavy, it sinks to the bottom, while everything that is not gold rises to the top. It is called "dross." It is skimmed off the top until nothing is left but pure gold. Without the heat, there is no pure gold. That is what Job is referring to. When God has tried (refined) me, I shall come forth as pure gold.

Let me close with one of my favorite quotes. It is from C. S. Lewis:

> Imagine yourself a living house. God comes in to rebuild that house. At first, perhaps, you can understand what He is doing. He is getting the drains right and stopping the leaks in the roof and so on. . . . But presently, He starts knocking the house about in a way that hurts abominably and does not seem to make sense. What on earth is He up to? The explanation is that He is building quite a different house

from the one you thought of . . . throwing out a new wing here, putting on an extra floor there, running up towers, making court-yards. You thought you were going to be made into a decent little cottage: but He is building a palace.

Speed Bump!

Slow down to be sure you've gotten the main points of this chapter.

Question   **Q1.** What does the Bible teach about the role of time in
                    spiritual growth?
Answer   **A1.** The Bible teaches that spiritual growth requires *time*,
                    just as physical growth does.

Q2. What does the Bible teach about the role of trials in spiritual growth?

A2. The Bible teaches that trials are used by God to make us spiritually insightful and *strong*.

Q3. What examples does the Bible give us of the role of time and trials?

A3. The Bible gives us many examples of spiritual leaders whose trials eventually produced spiritual *maturity*.

Fill in the Blank

Question   **Q1.** What does the Bible teach about the role of time in
                    spiritual growth?
Answer   **A1.** The Bible teaches that spiritual growth requires
                    _____, just as physical growth does.

Q2. What does the Bible teach about the role of trials in spiritual growth?

A2. The Bible teaches that trials are used by God to make us spiritually insightful and _____ .

Q3. What examples does the Bible give us of the role of time and trials?

A3. The Bible gives us many examples of spiritual leaders whose trials eventually produced spiritual _____ .

For Further Thought and Discussion

1. Do you have the feeling you ought to be more spiritually mature than you are by now? Do you think there is some possibility you just need more time?

2. Have you ever had the feeling that God was angry with you for an unknown reason, or punishing you for something you did not know about? What is the possibility that God is not angry or punishing you, but that He is just using something hard in your life to make you more mature?

3. What encouragement do you personally get from the examples of the biblical characters who grew strong through trials over time?

What If I Don't Believe?

If I don't realize that time and trials are both needed to bring me to spiritual maturity, I may conclude that Christianity isn't working for me, and quit. I may feel that God is angry with me, and give up because I don't know what I did wrong. If I don't understand that God uses time and trials in every Christian's life to makes them spiritually strong, I may wear out, burn out, or give up. I may miss the good that God wants to give me, because I don't understand His ways.

For Further Study

1. Scripture

- Psalm 119:67, 71, 75

- Luke 2:52

- 2 Corinthians 4:8–11, 16–18

- James 1:2–4

- Peter 2:18–21

2. Books

Where is God When It Hurts? Philip Yancey
Disappointment With God, Philip Yancey
Making Sense Out of Suffering, Peter Kreeft
The Problem of Pain, C. S. Lewis

Part Two:
Pursuing Spiritual Growth

Little faith will bring your soul to heaven; great faith
will bring heaven to your soul.
■ **Charles Haddon Spurgeon (1834–1892)**

How Does Faith Affect My Spiritual Growth?

Faith is a powerful thing. By faith, Jesus said, we could move mountains. That was a figure of speech, of course, but many personal mountains have been moved by faith. Faith is the foundation of the Christian life, and its importance cannot be overstated.

An old story tells about the man who fell over the side of a cliff and grabbed a small tree just before plunging many feet to his death below. As he hung there, he cried out for someone to help him, and a deep, booming voice came from everywhere.

"Do you trust me?"
The man said, "Who's that?"
The voice said, "It's the Lord. Do you trust me?"
The man said, "Yes, yes! Yes! I trust you! Help me!"
"Let go of the branch. I'll save you."
"What?" the man gasped.
"Let go of the branch," was the reply.
"Let go of the branch?" the man whimpered.
"Yes," the voice repeated.
The man was silent for several moments. Then he yelled, "Is anybody else up there?"

This is faith, or lack of it, at work. Faith determines our actions. We act on what we believe. We don't act on what we don't believe. If we believe the Bible, we act accordingly. When we don't act accordingly, it is because we don't believe the Bible. Therefore, properly understood, the opposite of obedience is not disobedience. The opposite of obedience is unbelief! (Hebrews 11:6).

In this chapter we learn that . . . **1.** Faith demands total commitment to God. **2.** Faith motivates the Christian to be totally obedient. **3.** Faith gives me the strength to persevere in the face of trials.

If the man on the cliff had believed God, he would have let go. It is as simple as that. Because he did not believe, he was unwilling to let go. The same is true with our Christian life. If God tells us to let go or to hang on, we obey if we believe Him. If we doubt, we do whatever we think will be best for us.

For example, a husband may be tired of his wife. She no longer pleases him. In fact, he has gotten to the point at which he can no longer stand the sight of her. He knows the Bible says that he should not divorce his wife, because he has no biblical grounds. If he went to the right person for counsel, he would be told to stay with his wife, and God would give him the grace and wisdom to work out the relationship. Otherwise he would be sinning, bring pain and heartache into his life that could be avoided, and even be subject to the discipline of the Lord (Hebrews 12:5–11). If the man believes that, he stays with his wife, works with the counselor, and trusts the Lord to give him the grace to have his relationship restored. If he doesn't, he files for divorce.

We all act on what we believe. Faith is everything in spiritual growth.

What Decision Does Faith Demand From Me?

Faith demands total commitment to God.

In a deeply insightful book, *Half Time*, Bob Buford tells of a defining moment when he was forced to determine what would be the driving force of his life. A strategic planning consultant told him of the time Coca-Cola was forced to answer the question, "What's in the box?" That is, if they could write only one thing in a box that would describe the primary purpose, the "mainspring" of their company, what would they write? After many hours of deliberation, the executives at Coca-Cola decided that "great taste" was what they would write in their box. As a result, they conducted tests to find a tastier formula than the original one and introduced "New Coke." In doing so, they stepped into a mine field of marketing debacles. America simply refused to accept the new product.

The planning consultant was called back to Coca-Cola to find out what went wrong. The consultant told them that they must have put the wrong thing in the box if they didn't like the results they got.

So they tried again, and after hours of new deliberation, came up with "American tradition" to put in the box. They discovered that pulling original Coca-Cola off the market was tampering with an American institution like apple pie, baseball, and motherhood. Finding the right word to put in the box enabled them to recover their momentum quickly after this near-disastrous blunder.

A person can have only one primary loyalty. Just as companies have to write something in the box that defines their driving force, so must individuals. Each of us must write something in the box, and there can be only one thing in the box. A person can have only one primary loyalty.

This same strategic planning consultant pushed Bob Buford, during a time of reassessment in his life, to determine what he would write in his box. Buford, a highly successful and wealthy businessman, had been living for the success of business. So he had to choose. Would he put "success" in the box, or would he put "Jesus"? He could only put one word in the box. Buford decided that if he could only put one word in the box, he would put "Jesus."

After that, he wrote:

> To put Christ in the box, I found, is actually a sign of contradiction, a paradox. To put Christ in the box is to break down the walls of the box and allow the power and grace of his life to invade every aspect of your own life. It follows the same wonderfully inverted logic as the ancient assertion that it is in giving that one received, in our weakness we are made strong, and in dying we are born to richer life (52).

Each of us must determine our main motivation in life. It will either be Jesus or something else. Writing Jesus in the box does not ensure that the rest of our life will go smoothly. It simply indicates what drives us, regardless of whether the road is bumpy or smooth.

Bob Buford learned this lesson when, shortly after he wrote "Jesus" in the box, his only child, a young man of great promise,

Bob's heir and successor to the family fortune and business, drowned in a swimming accident. Buford had a choice: to spit in the face of God, erase "Jesus" and put something else in the box, or to leave "Jesus" in the box and trust Him to help him survive the blow. He chose to leave Jesus in the box.

Why I Need to Know This

I need to know that faith demands total obedience. Otherwise, I might think that I can play around with half-hearted obedience to God and still experience the depth of spiritual life that God and I both want me to have. I need to know that if I truly believe God I will be totally obedient, and persevere in the face of trials.

When he spoke at a church two and a half weeks after they buried his son, Buford prayed,

God, you have given my life into my hands. I give it back to you. My time, my property, my life itself . . . knowing it is only an instant compared to my life with you in eternity. Father, to you I release the cares and concerns of this world, knowing you loved me enough to give your only Son in my behalf. I'm a sinner in need of a Savior and, once again, I accept what you have done for me as sufficient. In Jesus' name. Amen (58).

It was a tender and precious prayer that could only be prayed if "Jesus" were written in the box. If anything else were in the box, those words would not have come to him.

What is in your box? You must decide what you will believe, what will be your primary loyalty and driving motivation in life. Will it be Jesus or something else? The apostle Paul wrote in Romans 12:1–2,

Therefore, I urge you, brothers, in view of God's mercy, to offer your bodies as living sacrifices, holy and pleasing to God—this is your spiritual act of worship. Do not conform any longer to the pattern of this world, but be transformed by the renewing of your mind. Then you will be able to test and approve what God's will is—his good, pleasing and perfect will. (NIV)

We can only be living demonstrations of the goodness of God if we have first offered ourselves as a living sacrifice to Him.

What Motivation Does Faith Give Me?
Faith motivates the Christian to be totally obedient.

Faith has a profound effect on the Christian life in at least three areas: obedience, peace, and hope. Blaise Pascal, a 17th-century French philosopher, said (correctly, I believe):

All men seek happiness. This is without exception. Whatever different means they employ, they all tend to this end. The cause of some going to war, and of others avoiding it is the same desire in both, attending with different views. The will never takes the least step but to this objective. This is the motive of every man, even of those who hang themselves. (*Pensées* #425)

This is true because God has created us to desire our own well-being rather than our own suffering. Anything else would not be the "image of God."

This fact must be wedded to another for full understanding: "Everything God asks of us, He does so to give some good thing to us, or to keep some harm from us."

If it is true that all men desire their own happiness and never take the least step except to that end (even to those who hang themselves), and if we deeply believe that God only asks from us that which will give us some good or keep us from some harm, then we would never willfully disobey God!

Every road will either lead you closer to Christ or farther from Him.

Why would we? Disobedience would be masochistic (enjoying self-inflicted pain). When we come to the point in our lives that we wholeheartedly believe that to disobey God is simply to shoot ourselves in the foot, we become much less prone to disobedience and sin. Such a belief is a powerful incentive to godliness.

For example, suppose a person is tempted by pornography. The first illicit glimpses give an initial rush of excitement. Yet it does not satisfy. Mild pornography must lead either to repentance or harder pornography, which in turn must lead to repentance or the hardest pornography. Then, when the hardest pornography does not satisfy, the person must either repent or begin to act out the pornography. But when acting it out on a basic level does not satisfy, the person must either repent or eventually destroy himself. It is as James wrote in his epistle: "Then, when desire has conceived, it gives birth to sin; and when sin is full-grown, brings forth death" (1:15).

Every road goes somewhere. The road that begins with *Playboy*, if traveled to the end, will lead to emotional enslavement, perversion, abuse, and eventually death.

I don't mean that everyone who reads *Playboy* will kill himself. But the person must stop somewhere on the road first (which most people do) or he will get to the end of the road, which is destruction. God doesn't ask us to keep our minds and hearts pure to limit us. He does so to keep us from the self-destructive nature of impurity, and to make us able to enjoy holy intimacy with a marriage partner.

Let me give a less extreme (though more common than we might think) example of consumer debt. Unfortunately, many Christians are crippled with consumer debt because they have never learned to control their finances with God's principles. Many Christians are so strapped financially that they are unable to provide for the basics of life or prepare for the emergencies of life or to give to the ministries of life.

How do they get into such financial bondage? In many cases, they believe that material possessions will give them happiness. They believe that a bigger car or house, or fancier clothes or vacations, or better boats or jewelry will make them happy. And these things may, for the moment. But they do not give lasting peace, love, and joy. Nothing outside the will of God does.

These debt-ridden Christians may know that the Bible teaches you should support the work of the Lord, share with the disadvantaged, and prepare for your retirement, but they don't believe they will be happier right now by doing so. They think happiness lies in buying the next thing they want.

If they believed that they would be happier supporting the work of the Lord, sharing with the disadvantaged, and preparing for their retirement than they would by buying a new car or going on a fabulous vacation, they would give to others and save. If they are not giving to others and saving, they do not believe God.

The shrivelled soul is one that lives only for itself.

I really am from the same planet as you, and I admit that a new car or great vacation is certainly more pleasure-generating than donating my money to a charity or socking it away in an IRA. However, stingy and selfish people are never as happy in the long run as generous and compassionate people are. It shrivels the soul to live only for oneself. We were not made for that existence. And when we retire, if we do not have enough money put away we will come to the bitter realization that the fun we had twenty years earlier was not worth the poverty we must live in now.

We always obey our beliefs. The massive disobedience in the church today is rooted in massive unbelief. We do not believe that God's way is the only way to experience deep-seated, long-lasting peace, love, and joy. We go for the quick fix. We do not know or believe that sin is easier in the short run but harder in the long run, and that righteousness is harder in the short run, but easier in the long run. If we did, we would choose righteousness every time.

In this way faith gives us strength to obey.

What Strength Does Faith Give Me?

Faith gives me the strength to persevere in the face of trials.

Sometimes when life hauls off and socks us right in the stomach, we often ask "Why me?" or "Where is God?" We may feel like giving up when God doesn't make sense. Why doesn't He take better care of His children? Why do the innocent suffer? Where is God when it hurts? Why do bad things happen to good people? Why me? Why this? Why now?

But faith steps in like a mother settling a rowdy group of children and quiets the riot of questions. No, there are not always answers to our questions. But faith tells us several key things. First, faith reminds us that God is all good and all powerful. He can be trusted in spite of the pain. Being all powerful, He can do anything He wants, and if He is all good, He will never do anything bad.

Faith tells us that God can use bad things for good. Certainly bad things happen to us, and we don't know why God allows them. But Romans 8:28 says, "And we know that all things work together for good to those who love God, to those who are the called according to His purpose." It does not say that all things are good, but that God will work all things together for good, giving back beauty for ashes.

Faith tells us that trials can make us strong—that we can become more through trials than we can become without them.

Just as an athlete cannot triumph without pushing his body beyond its comfort zone, just as a musician cannot master his instrument without hour-to-years of rigorous practice, just as a scholar cannot become an expert without judicious yet creative investigation, so a Christian cannot mature without being forced beyond his spiritual comfort zone. Only as God stretches us beyond our present capacity can that capacity be enlarged.

Trials take us beyond our spiritual comfort zone. They are unpleasant, they may cause confusion and uncertainty; and they may even create a desire to rebel or quit. Jesus Himself **Trials take us beyond our spiritual comfort zone.** prayed that He might be spared the suffering that was prepared for Him. But submitting Himself to the will of God, He gave Himself to the Cross when God did not exempt Him from it. Jesus is our example. We must all go through suffering. But God will with the temptation provide a way of escape that we will be able to bear it (1 Corinthians 10:13), and will use the trials to make us mature and complete (James 1:2–4).

Faith tells us that our suffering will be rewarded in heaven many times over.

When you look back over your life at the significant things that you have accomplished, usually they were harder than you thought they were going to be, but more rewarding than you dreamed they could be. When I was playing basketball in high school and college, the daily practice sessions were nearly terminal. In high school our coach ran us until I thought my lungs would spontaneously combust. I thought my heart would hammer itself out of my chest cavity. I thought my legs would buckle from utter exhaustion. I often wanted to quit. I thought, *this isn't worth it!* But my senior year, our very small high school was one of the last teams remaining in a statewide basketball tournament that was not divided into classes. Davids played Goliaths all the time, and (to switch metaphors), Cinderellas often emerged. We were one of the Cinderellas that year. How was it? Wonderful! Was it worth it? Yes! Would I do it again, now that I know the reward? Yes!

This simple illustration can be extrapolated heavenward. The apostle Paul says that "the sufferings of this present time are not worthy to be compared with the glory which shall be revealed in us" (Romans 8:18). Now I know that you are thinking, *Heaven is going to have to be pretty good to make up for what I have gone/am going through.* And you are right. If the sufferings of this time are not worthy to be compared with the glory to be revealed to us in heaven, then heaven must be spectacular beyond our ability even to envision or comprehend. Imagine the horrors of being a prisoner of war. Think about someone being beaten and imprisoned in China for proclaiming the gospel. Put yourself in the shoes of a pastor who watches his family die at the hands of tribal enemies in Africa. The horrors are unspeakable. They are unimaginable except to those close to them. Are those sufferings not worthy to be compared to the glory to be revealed to us in heaven? The Bible says no! How good will heaven have to be in order for such sufferings to pale in comparison? We cannot even imagine.

But faith tells us it is so. Faith calmly assures us that

even though our outward man is perishing, yet the inward man is being renewed day by day. For our light affliction, which is but for a moment, is working for us a far more exceeding and eternal weight of glory, while we do not look at the things which are seen, but at the things which are not seen. For the things which are seen are temporary, but the things which are not seen are eternal (2 Corinthians 4:16–18).

Faith, then, in addition to motivating us to be obedient, gives us the strength to keep going in the face of suffering and trials.

Conclusion

Corrie ten Boom was a Dutch lady who was imprisoned in a German concentration camp for helping to hide Jews during the persecution of the Nazi holocaust. In the introduction to her book, *Tramp for the Lord*, she wrote:

Looking back over the years of my life, I can see the working of a divine pattern which is the way of God with His children. When I was in a prison camp in Holland during the war, I often prayed, "Lord, never let the enemy put me in a German concentration camp." God answered "no" to that prayer. Yet in the German camp, with all its horror, I found many prisoners who had never heard of Jesus Christ. If God had not used my sister Betsie and me to bring them to Him, they would never have heard of Him. Many died, or were killed, but many died with the name of Jesus on their lips. They were well worth all our suffering. Faith is like radar which sees through the fog—the reality of things at a distance that the human eye cannot see.

> My life is but a weaving, between my God and me,
> I do not choose the colors, He worketh steadily,
> Oftimes He weaveth sorrow, and I in foolish pride,
> Forget He sees the upper, and I the underside.
> Not till the loom is silent, and shuttles cease to fly,
> Will God unroll the canvas and explain the reason why.
> The dark threads are as needful in the skillful Weaver's hand,
> As the threads of gold and silver in the pattern He has planned.

Although the threads of my life have often seemed knotted, I know, by faith, that on the other side of the embroidery there is a crown (11–12).

Faith is central to spiritual growth. With it, we believe, we obey, we persevere to the glory of God and the benefit of humanity. Without it, we doubt, we disobey, we quit to the reproach of God and the ruin of humanity.

Faith sees what the human eye cannot.

Speed Bump!

Slow down to be sure you've gotten the main points of this chapter.

*Q*uestion
*A*nswer

Q1. What decision does faith demand from me?

A1. Faith demands total *commitment* to God.

Q2. What motivation does faith give me?

A2. Faith motivates the Christian to be totally *obedient*.

Q3. What strength does faith give me?

A3. Faith gives me the strength to *persevere* in the face of trials.

Fill in the Blank

*Q*uestion
*A*nswer

Q1. What decision does faith demand from me?

A1. Faith demands total _____ to God.

Q2. What motivation does faith give me?

A2. Faith motivates the Christian to be totally _____ .

Q3. What strength does faith give me?

A3. Faith gives me the strength to _____ in the face of trials.

For Further Thought and Discussion

1. Have you ever come to a point of total commitment in your life? If not, what do you think keeps you from it? Have you made the decision to be totally committed and then realized later that you had reneged on the commitment? What do you think a person should do about it when that happens?

2. Does it seem right to you that "the opposite of obedience is unbelief"? Can you think of an example of disobedience in your own life that you realize is rooted in unbelief? Explain.

3. Can you think of an example in which faith helped you to persevere in the face of a problem, trial, or suffering? How does that encourage you to do the same next time?

What If I Don't Believe?

If I don't believe that faith demands total commitment to God, I am liable to live in slipshod obedience, possibly fooling myself into thinking that I am living an acceptable Christian life. Total commitment is hard enough to maintain when I believe in the necessity for it. If I don't believe in the necessity for total commitment, I will most certainly not make it.

If I don't trust God and believe in the integrity of His instructions and commandments, I will often not have the strength to do the difficult things I ought to do, nor the strength to keep going in the face of tough times. If I don't have faith, my Christian life is going to be discouraging and defeated.

For Further Study

1. Scripture

- Romans 12:1–2

- 1 Corinthians 10:13

- 2 Corinthians 4:16–18

- Hebrews 11:6
- James 1:2–4

2. Book

Knowing God, James Packer

Sin is a boomerang. You throw it in pleasure;
it comes back to you in pain.

How Does Entrenched Sin Hinder Spiritual Growth?

Not long ago, I read major sections of Charles Dickens' *A Christmas Carol*, and I could not get over how good it was. I have seen several of its film versions and thought they were wonderful, but the book is better than the film. The reader learns more about the characters' thoughts and feelings. Reading elicits a deeper personal response than watching a film.

The book begins, "Old Marley was as dead as a door nail. To begin with, there was no doubt whatever about that. This must be distinctly understood or nothing wonderful can come of the story I am going to relate."

After Marley's death, on Christmas Eve, Scrooge retires to his dark and melancholy home to gobble a bowl of gruel and go to bed. As he relaxes for a moment by the fireplace in his bedroom, he hears the sounds of a man lumbering laboriously down the hallway toward his closed bedroom door, apparently dragging a heavy chain. Scrooge is terrified as a dreadful apparition passes through the closed door of his bedroom and stands before him. To Scrooge's utter amazement, the apparition bears a ghostly resemblance to his former stingy partner, Marley. Dickens writes:

> The same face, the very same, Marley in his pigtail, usual Waistcoat, tights and boots, the chain he drew was clasped about his middle, it was long and wound about him like a tail. It was made of cash boxes, teas, pad locks, ledgers, deeds and heavy purses wrought in steel. His body was transparent so that Scrooge could see the two buttons on his coat behind. Scrooge had often heard it said that Marley had no bowels, but he did not believe it till now.

Then Scrooge observed, "You're fettered. Tell me why?" To which Marley replied,

I wear the chain I forged in life. I made it link by link, yard by yard. I girded it of my own free will and of my own free will I wore it. Is its pattern strange to you or would you know the weight and length of the coil you bear yourself? [Your chain] was heavy and as full and as long as this seven Christmas Eves ago. You have labored on it since. It is a ponderous chain. I am here tonight to warn you that you have yet a chance and hope of escaping my fate, a chance and hope of my procuring, Ebenezer.

Scrooge was unaware that he had any chain about him. He could neither see nor feel it. But Marley assured him it was there, and if Scrooge died before doing something to remove it, it would be just as real to him after death as Marley's was that moment.

In this chapter we learn that . . .

1. Entrenched sin is chronic sin that a Christian has a difficult time getting consistent victory over.
2. Sin usually gets entrenched when we indulge small sins which gradually become bigger ones.
3. Entrenched sin can debilitate the Christian and even destroy the one who does not escape.
4. The Christian can gain victory over entrenched sin by repenting and receiving the grace of God.

Just as Marley and Scrooge forged chains of bondage in *A Christmas Carol*, so each of us forges chains of bondage in this life. As invisible as Scrooge's chains, they are just as ponderous, just as binding, just as tormenting as Marley's. Each of us—Satan sees to it—struggles with entrenched sin. Some of our chains are small and some are lengthy and weighty, but each of us has a chain. We live in a fallen world, we are born corrupted by sin, we learn bad habits, we are deceived—aided and abetted by the devil—so that I doubt if any of us is entirely free from entrenched sin.

Surely the drug-addicted prostitute is more deeply entrenched in sin than the widow who struggles with moderate overeating. But each of us struggles with entrenched sin, and it limits us from growing spiritually unless we learn how to deal with it.

What Is an Entrenched Sin?

Entrenched sin is chronic sin that a Christian has a difficult time getting consistent victory over.

In the summer 1996 issue of *Leadership,* an anonymous pastor told of his experience with entrenched sin:

> My wife had risen early to work out at the local health club. I was still asleep.
>
> Since my car was parked behind hers in the driveway, she decided to drive mine. The windshield was frosted, so she began rummaging in my car for an ice scraper. When she reached under the seat, she pulled out a video—a porn video.
>
> Not knowing what it was—though she knew by the title it wasn't work related—she came into the house and shoved it into the VCR. Minutes later she ran into our bedroom. I awoke to her sobbing, "What is this!?"
>
> My secret was out.
>
> Before that memorable morning, I had been renting hard-core porno movies for a year and a half. The downward spiral began in college; it began by regularly thumbing through magazines like *Playboy* and *Penthouse.* Marriage didn't help. In fact, it provided more opportunities to be alone, when I was on the road or when my wife was at work.
>
> In one sense, though, I felt strange relief at my wife's discovery. I had wanted to be rid of my sin for so long. ("Alone with My Lust," 50).

This is entrenched sin, a sin that the person did not want any more, but on his own was not able to overcome.

All of us have entrenched sins, though fortunately they are not usually as extreme as this one. We might be entrenched in the sin of

- overeating

- gossiping

- anger

- too much or the wrong kind of television (lust? laziness?)

- worry

- sarcasm
- bitterness
- materialism
- pride
- laziness
- envy
- alcohol, drugs, tobacco
- or _____ (fill in the blank).

On a continuum, entrenched sin may be anywhere from minor to life-controlling. But I believe that our fallen world combines with our indwelling sin and the presence of the devil and his demons to make sure none of us is without entrenched sin unless we have dealt with it biblically. And even then, I believe, it always presents a temptation and danger. Like a tiger in a cage, as long as you face it and control it, you survive, but turn your back on it for a moment, lose your concentration, make a foolish move, and it is there again to eat you alive.

Why I Need to Know This

I need to know this in order to recognize entrenched sin in my life in order to escape it. I need to know how sin gets entrenched so that I can avoid it before it becomes entrenched. Finally, I need to know the power of repentance and confession, and to believe that the Lord will give me victory over entrenched sin.

Scripture talks about entrenched sin in 2 Corinthians 10:4–5:

For the weapons of our warfare are not carnal [of the flesh] but mighty in God for pulling down strongholds, casting down arguments and every high thing that exalts itself against the knowledge of God.

The apostle Paul referred to a "stronghold," which is a type of fortress, well defended and hard to overthrow. Strongholds can be defeated, but not easily.

How Does Sin Get Entrenched?

Sin usually gets entrenched when we indulge small sins which gradually become bigger ones.

Sin usually gets entrenched the same way a brick wall gets laid—one brick at a time. We indulge in a small sin, thinking it won't hurt. Left to itself, it would not be so damaging. But when combined with others becomes so strong it cannot be broken. As Ecclesiastes says, "A cord of three strands is not easily broken" (4:12), though a cord of one strand might be. We weave and braid our sins together until they are so strong we feel powerless to help ourselves.

In our previous example, the pastor entrenched in pornography began by flipping through *Playboy* and *Penthouse* magazines. The pornography "snack" developed into appetite and grew to movies and hard-core videos. It nearly wrecked his marriage. Most immorality and sin is the cumulative weight of small indulgences and minor compromises which add up and grow. Like a St. Bernard puppy that we carry home in our arms but which, when we keep feeding it, soon becomes too big to carry, so it is with sin. Initially, perhaps, we can carry it, but if we keep feeding it, it soon outgrows us.

Sin can also get entrenched through shock effect. When a young boy finds a magazine from a nudist camp hidden under his teen-age brother's mattress, it can have a powerful, drawing effect toward pornography that the younger child may never have allowed to happen through the one-small-sin-at-a-time approach.

When a daughter is sexually abused by a trusted relative, a similar thing can happen—a knowledge of, an interest in, an intimacy level with a sin that she is nowhere near prepared to deal with. The combined shame and guilt along with the drawing power that sexual experience has can entrench a girl in sin that, if she had never been abused, she might never have allowed to happen through the one-small-sin-at-a-time approach.

Regardless of how we get them, regardless of whether they are nagging, little things, or life-controlling addictions, we all have entrenched sin. Satan sees to it.

Why Is Entrenched Sin So Bad?

Entrenched sin can debilitate the Christian and even destroy the one who does not escape.

Everyone agrees that entrenched sin is bad and that it hinders spiritual growth. When we properly understand what sin is, we will hate it and want to avoid it at all costs. All sin is ruination and destruction of good. Sin is bad not because God says so, but rather God says so because He wants to reveal it for what it truly is.

There are at least three major reasons why entrenched sin, or any sin, is so bad.

Sin Destroys the Picture of God

God wants Christians to reflect Him, to magnify Him, and to glorify Him. But we must understand why. Certainly God is deserving of our glorification, but there is more to it than that. God is not a cosmic egomaniac who wants humans to grovel at His feet with stooped shoulders and an ingratiating grin, wringing their hands and constantly saying "yes, sir," and "no, sir," and "whatever you wish, sir."

God wants Christians to glorify Him, because in doing so, we give an accurate picture to the world of what God is like. Then, people who don't know Him will want to know Him because of what they see of Him in us. We are His reputation.

When we live in sin, the world does not get an accurate picture of what God is like, and others will not want to know Him because they don't know what He is like. Sin among Christians drives non-Christians away from God. That is a terrible thing to do, and ought to make us determined either to deal with our sin, or never testify that we are Christians.

Sin Destroys Human Relationships

Relationships make life worthwhile, not money, not fame, not excitement. There is nothing wrong with money, fame, or excitement in and of themselves. But they will not support a meaningful life if placed at the core of that life. Relationships are the essence of every meaningful life, and the other things must be placed around that core.

Someone has said to be careful whom you marry, for from that one decision may come 90 percent of the happiness or misery that you will experience in life. That may be an overstatement, but the point is well made. Our marriage, our children, our coworkers, our neighbors, our fellow church members, our extended family members all combine to be perhaps the major source of joy or misery in life.

It is easier to hear the whispers of sin than the cries of the Holy Spirit.

Relationships are so hard to enjoy. Why? Because sin sits on our shoulder and whispers, "Self. Self is more important. You must look out for yourself; you must satisfy yourself. It is more blessed to receive than to give. Do unto others before others do unto you. Look out for number one."

Those whisperings sow the seeds of destruction for any relationship. The Holy Spirit sits on our other shoulder and cries, "Others. Others. Do not merely look out for your own interests, but be interested in the welfare of others. Do to others as you would have others do to you. Love your neighbor as yourself."

The tendency toward sin that we still have (Romans 7) plus the selfish nature of our society often cause us to hear the whispers of sin more clearly than the urgings of the Holy Spirit. But selfishness destroys relationships. Proverbs 15:1, for example, says, "A soft answer turns away wrath, but a harsh word stirs up anger." So when in the process of trying to help our spouse plant some flowers we accidentally destroy one of them, and our spouse flares up, "Be careful, for crying out loud, you just ruined that petunia!" the Holy Spirit whispers, "Forgive. Return a soft answer." And if we do, wrath slinks away and the relationship is strengthened. At the same time, sin screams, "Don't take that guff. You were only trying to help, so if it isn't appreciated, tell your spouse to go jump in the lake. Then you go back in the house!" And if you do, the harsh word will stir up anger, and the relationship will be weakened.

As these kinds of things happen over and over in the relationship, the relationship will either flourish or die. When I was in seminary, a vast Southern Bell building stood close to campus. Over ten stories tall with nearly the perimeter of an entire city block, it was constructed entirely of bricks. My mind reeled to imagine all those bricks! That whole building was built one brick at a time. And many walls in relationships are built, one brick, one argument, one unresolved misunderstanding at a time, until the wall is so high it seems insurmountable.

In his book *Not the Way It's Supposed to Be,* Cornelius Plantiga writes,

> Sin distorts our character . . . until [it] becomes a center of attack on others or of defection or neglect. Bad enough if we offend others involuntarily—by boorish insensitivity to their feelings, for example, or by an alienating form of complacency. We may not want these character flaws; in fact, we may not even know that we have them. But if our victims know that we have hurt them consciously, deliberately, even serenely, their attitude toward us is not merely rueful, as it would normally be if we had harmed them by accident. Their attitude is not just sorrowful, as it normally is when nature catches people in its great machinery. Instead, our victims face us indignantly. For they know we have violated them with something powerfully and peculiarly personal. We have *willingly* hurt them. We have done it on purpose (2–3).

When that happens, the relationship is ruptured. Only humility and skill can repair it. Sin is bad because it damages and destroys relationships, the very things that make life worth living.

Sin Destroys the Sinner

Finally, sin is bad because it destroys the sinner. All sin boomerangs and strikes a lethal blow to the very one who throws it. In Proverbs 14:1 we read, "The wise woman builds her house, but the foolish pulls it down with her hands." She does not pull it down purposely; she does not want to pull down the house. But she insists on her foolishness, and the house collapses as a consequence. Sin boomerangs.

Again, in Proverbs we read, "Whoever commits adultery with a woman lacks understanding; He who does so destroys his own soul" (6:32). The person does not want to destroy his own soul. He just wants to commit adultery. But with the adultery comes the destruction of his soul. Sin boomerangs.

The adulterer destroys his home, the homosexual contracts AIDS, the thief is arrested, the angry person loses his job, the lazy person cannot make ends meet, the materialistic person files bankruptcy, the hypocritical person loses the respect of his children, the alcoholic dies of liver disease, and on and on it goes. Sin boomerangs. Sin damages and eventually destroys the sinner.

How Can the Christian Gain Victory Over Entrenched Sin?

The Christian can gain victory over entrenched sin by repenting and receiving the grace of God.

In his book *Rediscovering Holiness,* James Packer makes this powerful observation: "Only through constant and deepening repentance can we sinners *maintain our souls in health*" (149). Repentance of sin is the starting point for all victory over entrenched sin. We must admit that we are entrenched in sin, we must admit our powerlessness to escape without the grace of God, and we must resolutely turn from our sin as best we can. That is step number one.

Beyond this, of course, one must pray. We must call on God to help and deliver us. We must flee to His arms, as it were, so that He can save us. This is serious praying. When we talk about praying, we think more on the level of "now I lay me down to sleep," or "God is great, God is good and we thank Him for this food." But "Lord, help me!" is as serious, earnest, and legitimate praying as can be done. I think of Peter who had the audacity to leave the boat and walk out on the water to meet Jesus, but then started getting wet feet (excuse me) and began to sink. He cried out, "Lord, save me!" and the Bible says that immediately Jesus reached out His hand to save him (Matthew 14:31). Our prayer for deliverance from entrenched sin is no less valid a prayer.

In Ephesians 6:18, the apostle Paul links success in spiritual warfare (an element of spiritual warfare resides in all entrenched sin) to "prayer and supplication in the Spirit." Part of taking up our spiritual armor in Ephesians is focused and concentrated prayer, not only by the person engaged in spiritual warfare, but by those who pray for him or her. Of course, other spiritual warfare measures may need to be taken, including a serious study of the spiritual armor in Ephesians 6:10–18 (as a beginning point for this, see *What You Need to Know About Spiritual Warfare* in this series).

Beyond those critical steps, some specific additional measures may need to be taken to bolster an individual's strength to overcome entrenched sin. The first of these measures can be used to keep from becoming entrenched in sin and the latter ones can be used to get out of entrenched sin.

Maintain the basics. Often those who descend into entrenched sin can look back to lapses in the basic Christian disciplines of going to church, reading the Bible, praying, and spending time with other Christians. The isolation from the basic building-block activities of a healthy Christian life is often the beginning point for entrenched sin.

Solitude for healthy self-examination is an extremely helpful measure which very few people take. Ancient Israel had one day of rest each week, several weeks of rest each year, and one year of rest every seven years to give them enough solitude and focused time to keep their spiritual lives healthy.

Each of us ought to take periodic getaways of an afternoon, or overnight, or week or so, sometimes alone and sometimes with a spouse, to have time to speak to and listen to God, to hear that "still small voice" that so easily gets overwhelmed by the noise and pace of everyday living.

Guard the environment. I heard the story of a little girl who was instructed not to eat any of the cookies her mother was baking that morning since they were for company that night, and the mother put them in the pantry. Later in the afternoon, the mother found that the little girl was missing. "Susie!" her mother called. "Where are you?"

Susie called back, "I'm in the pantry."

"What are you doing in the pantry?" her mother asked.

Susie replied, "I'm fighting temptation."

Now, the place to fight temptation was not in the pantry, but in the living room beside her mother. The same is true with each of us. When we do not guard our environment, we more easily fall into temptation, and after repeated occurrences, descend into entrenched sin. For example, if you are tempted by alcohol, don't keep alcohol in the house. If you struggle with smoking, don't keep cigarettes in the house. If you struggle with pornography, don't have cable television channels that put you at risk. If you struggle with anything, don't have it in easy reach. Keep the source of your temptation as far away from you as you can.

Be decisive with small things. We can handle things when they are small. But small things grow when they are fed, and soon the small things become bigger than we are. So we must deal decisively with small things. Everyone is vulnerable to sexual immorality, and we are swimming in a cesspool of temptation in modern American culture. It flatters a pastor, for example, to receive attention from an attractive woman who obviously admires him and hangs on his every word when at the last board meeting the deacons didn't admire him and stomped on his every word. She may send notes of appreciation harmless enough in themselves, but often expressions of respect sprout into expressions of admiration which bloom into expressions of affection, and pretty soon a bond is formed which, if not broken, will only set both parties up for sexual immorality. We must deal decisively with small things while they are still small.

Our thoughts are the threads we use to weave the fabric of our lives. Thread by thread, thought by thought, we create our own destiny. Paul said in Philippians 4:8, "Whatever is honorable, whatever is right, whatever is pure, whatever is lovely, whatever is of good repute, if there is any excellence and if anything worthy of praise, let your mind dwell on these things" (NASB). Any time we allow our mind to dwell on things that do not pass the test of this passage, we are setting ourselves up for trouble.

Be spiritually accountable to someone. There ought to be someone or even a small group in your life with whom you can be totally authentic and transparent. There ought to be other Christians in your life in whom you can confide and to whom you have given the freedom to ask you personal and intimate questions, especially if they notice anything suspicious. They ought to ask questions such as, "How are you doing?" and if the answers seem vague or evasive, then probe even deeper.

I heard one time of a set of questions that a group of pastors asked each other each week. I thought they were great questions, and everyone ought to have a group of men for a man, or women for a woman, where these kinds of questions can be asked. Some of these questions would need to be revised a little if the people involved in the group were not pastors.

- Have you been with a woman this week in a way that was or might be seen as inappropriate or in poor judgment?

- Have you been above reproach with your finances this week?

- Have you exposed yourself to any explicit material (anything inappropriate) this week?

- Have you been faithful to spend time in the Scriptures and prayer on a daily basis this week?

- Have you fulfilled the mandate of your calling this week?

- Have you spent adequate time with your family this week?

- Have you just lied to me?

Many people have found Christian Twelve-Step programs helpful. Though the format is often abused, it can be very helpful if led by spiritually mature and insightful Christians.

Visualize the ultimate consequences. Perhaps the single most effective tool I have found in avoiding and breaking besetting sin is to visualize the ultimate end of the sinful activity, and to ask myself if I am willing to pay the ultimate price for that sin. If not, I must turn around.

As an illustration, there are several gates in the ancient wall around Old Jerusalem. Several of the gates have interesting names. One is called the Dung Gate because the road from that gate led to the garbage dump. The Damascus Gate gives access to the road that leads to Damascus. The road from the Joppa Gate goes to Joppa. If you don't want to go to the garbage dump, there is no reason to go out the Dung Gate. If you do, you **All sin ultimately leads to destruction and death.** must either turn around or else end up at the garbage dump. If you don't want to go to Damascus, there is no reason to go out the Damascus Gate because if you do, you must either turn around or you will end up at Damascus. If you don't want to go to Joppa, don't go out the Joppa Gate.

The same is true of sin. All sin, if followed to its ultimate conclusion, leads to destruction and death. If you don't want destruction and death, you must either not go out the "Sin Gate" or else you must turn around. And the farther down the road you get, the harder it is to turn around. All roads to sin slant downhill, so it is easy to walk them, and very difficult to climb back up.

For example, if I am tempted to be dishonest, I ask myself if I am dishonest this time, what will keep me from being dishonest a second time? If I am dishonest a second time, what will keep me from developing the habit of dishonesty? If I develop the habit of dishonesty, what will keep me from eventually doing something illegal and winding up in prison? If I don't want to end up in prison, there is no reason to be dishonest the first time, because I must either turn around or end up in prison.

Another helpful example is in the area of sexual temptation. Whenever I am tempted to give in to sexual temptation (even in comparatively little matters such as paying attention to provocative TV commercials or magazine advertisements or movies with steamy scenes), I visualize being in the city of Old Jerusalem debating whether or not to go out the Sin Gate, knowing that it leads only one place: destruction. If I don't want to go there, there is no reason to go out the gate. The farther down the road I get before I turn around, the harder it is to turn around and get back. As Benjamin Franklin once said, "it is easier to deny the first illicit desire than to fulfill all the rest that would follow it."

Then, I think of specific things that would follow by giving in to the sin.

- I would personally spit in God's face.

- I would publicly kick dirt in His face.

- I would have to explain it when I get to heaven.

- I would devastate my wife and ruin my marriage.

- I would ruin all the wonderful relationships that are built around my marriage.

- I would lose my reputation.

- I would lose my ability to make a living.

- I would give up the satisfaction of being a minister, which is the only thing I find ultimately fulfilling.

- I would bury myself in guilt and remorse.

- I would discourage others from becoming a Christian.

- I might get a sexually transmitted disease.

- I would destroy another woman's life.

I have never, *never* seen a pastor fall into sin who was better off for it afterward—not nationally prominent figures who have fallen, nor obscure men who have fallen. I have never seen one who was richer, more satisfied, happier, traveled in a better circle of friends, or was more fulfilled. It *always* ends in disaster, heartache, and grief.

One of my professors in seminary told the story of this potentially great preacher or that particularly gifted minister who fell into sexual sin and will never be in the ministry again. One of the motivations of my life is never to be the subject of one of those stories.

Another motivation for me is to realize that if holiness is on the letter A and adultery is on the letter Z, I would never jump from A to Z. Never. I simply wouldn't do it. But I would move from A to B. I know. I have done it many times. I would move from B to C. I might even move from C to D. *I find that, no matter where I am on the alphabet, I am always capable of moving one letter to the right.* Well, if I am always capable of moving one letter to the right, I am capable eventually of committing adultery. Therefore I cannot take lightly moving from A to B, or B to C. If I ever got to Y, I am certain I would say, "Oh, what's the difference?" and I would jump right over to Z! So the trick is staying away from Y! To stay away from Y, I must stay away from X and W, and so on. I must have the mind-set that I will not move to the right. When I stumble, I must repent immediately and move back to A. I live under the constant realization that I am capable of falling into sexual immorality if I am not eternally vigilant about my place in the alphabet and which direction I'm moving.

When an alluring image tempts me, I try to imagine that the seductive image is a mask covering the rotted skeleton of death and destruction.

Everyone must ask himself, "What do I want out of life?" Then, he must ask himself, "Am I willing to pay the price?" No one would say, "I want misery, heartache, shame, grief, and guilt out of life." No one. So if we don't, we must deal ruthlessly with sin! We must master it, or it will master us.

Conclusion

In J.R.R. Tolkien's book, *The Hobbit*, there was no one seemingly more invincible than Smaug, the mighty dragon. But then that un-

likely hero, Bilbo Bagins, found one small weak spot in Smaug's un-
derbelly. That information, in the hands of a skilled marksman, was
all it took to seal the doom of the presumptuous dragon. Unaware of
his weakness and underestimating his opponents, Smaug failed to
protect himself. An arrow pierced his heart, and the dragon was
felled.

An exciting story with a happy ending. But when it's a Christian
leader felled, the ending is not so happy. It's tragic. The Evil One
knows only too well the weak spots of the most mighty Christian
warriors, not to mention the rest of us. He isn't one to waste his ar-
rows, bounding them harmlessly off the strongest plates of our spiritual armor. His aim is deadly, and it is at our points of greatest vulner-
ability that he will most certainly attack (*Leadership*, Summer 1996, 53).

Entrenched sin is a fact in the Christian life, and we must
learn to deal with it effectively or we will never experience the
spiritual growth we long for. Worse yet, it may be our downfall,
taking us from mere frustration and stagnation to tragedy.

Speed Bump!

Slow down to be sure you've gotten the main points of this chapter.

Question   **Q1.**   What is an entrenched sin?

Answer   **A1.**   Entrenched sin is *chronic* sin that a Christian has a
                     difficult time getting consistent victory over.

Q2.   How does sin get entrenched?

A2.   Sin usually gets entrenched when we indulge small sins which
         gradually become bigger ones.

Q3.   Why is entrenched sin so bad?

A3.   Entrenched sin can *debilitate* the Christian and even destroy the one
         who does not escape.

Q4.   How can the Christian gain victory over entrenched sin?

A4.   The Christian can gain victory over entrenched sin by *repenting* and
         receiving the grace of God.

Fill in the Blank

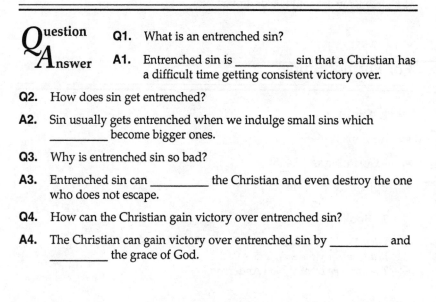

Question **Q1.** What is an entrenched sin?

Answer **A1.** Entrenched sin is _____ sin that a Christian has a difficult time getting consistent victory over.

Q2. How does sin get entrenched?

A2. Sin usually gets entrenched when we indulge small sins which _____ become bigger ones.

Q3. Why is entrenched sin so bad?

A3. Entrenched sin can _____ the Christian and even destroy the one who does not escape.

Q4. How can the Christian gain victory over entrenched sin?

A4. The Christian can gain victory over entrenched sin by _____ and _____ the grace of God.

For Further Thought and Discussion

1. Some entrenched sin, such as addiction to alcohol, drugs, or pornography, is very obvious. Other entrenched sin, such as gossip, worry, or materialism, can be much more subtle. Of the two types of entrenched sin, which do you think is the more prevalent in the church? Which do you think is the most harmful overall?

2. Have you seen anyone who was destroyed (perhaps not literally, but figuratively) by entrenched sin? What lessons did you learn from observing it?

3. What do you think is the most important thing a person can do to avoid getting entrenched in sin?

What If I Don't Believe?

If I don't believe in the reality and power of entrenched sin, I run a dangerous risk of getting trapped by it. If I don't take the steps necessary to avoid becoming entrenched, or if entrenched, don't take the steps necessary to be freed, my life could be destroyed.

For Further Study

1. Scripture

- Romans 7:14–8:1
- 2 Corinthians 10:4–5
- Ephesians 6:10–18

2. Books

What You Need to Know About Spiritual Warfare, Max Anders
Rediscovering Holiness, James Packer
The Bondage Breaker, Neil Anderson

When we talk of a man doing anything for God or giving anything to God, I will tell you what it is really like. It is like a small child going to its father and saying, "Daddy, give me six-pence to buy you a present." Of course, the father does, and he is pleased with the child's present.
■ C. S. Lewis

9

How Does Ministering to Others Help Me Grow Spiritually?

Corrie ten Boom, a Dutch woman who ministered to Jews during World War II and was imprisoned in a German concentration camp as reward for her efforts, had a very busy, worldwide ministry after the war. She described herself as a tramp for the Lord, traveling anywhere she felt the Lord leading her, to share the message of forgiveness and healing in Jesus. One time she heard of a lady in Russia who typed copies of the Bible and other Christian literature, including her books, and gave the copies to people who could not get copies any other way. As a way of recognizing the efforts of this elderly lady and to say thank you, she visited her (incognito, since this was during the period of Communist oppression in the Soviet Union). When Corrie arrived at the lady's apartment, she found her bent and twisted from multiple sclerosis, propped up by pillows so she wouldn't fall over. She writes about the experience in her book, *Tramp for the Lord:*

> She raised her right hand, slowly, in jerks. It was the only part of her body she could control and with her gnarled and deformed knuckles she caressed my face. I reached over and kissed the index finger of that hand, for it was with this one finger that she had so long glorified God.

> Her husband helped her in this tedious endeavor. He would put an ancient black typewriter in front of her on a small table and then, with that remarkable finger, she would begin to type.

All day and far into the night she would type. She translated [portions of the Bible and] Christian books into Russian, Latvian, and the language of her people. Always using just that one finger—peck . . . peck . . . peck— she typed out the pages (175–176).

We marvel at the vision, the commitment, the dedication this woman had to her task. She chose something she was able to do, and she did it, overcoming odds that move us deeply to read about. We would all excuse her with ready understanding if she did nothing with her Christian faith. After all, she had a near-perfect excuse. Instead, with her one finger, she rose to heights of heavenly glory that few of us will ever know.

Yet this level of commitment ought not to be so rare. Certainly our dedication to some of our obligations does not seem as heroic as typing all night with one finger. We may have to change diapers for two preschoolers, cook for four teenagers, hold down a job as well as keep house as a single parent, or some other rather mundane-seeming thing. If that is what God has called us to, it is as important as what this lady was doing.

In this chapter we learn that . . .

1. The commands of Christ, the teaching of Scripture, and the needs around us demand that we accept the challenge of ministering to others.
2. Outreach stimulates spiritual growth by stretching the Christian beyond his present level and bringing about learning, maturation, and fulfillment.
3. The Christian is responsible for evangelism, edification, and humanitarianism.
4. We remain motivated for the sacrifice of outreach by remembering it is an obligation because of what Christ and others have done for us.

But how many Christians have *no* ministry? How many Christians coast through life as invisible Christians in the workplace and passive Christians at church, neither serving nor giving? How many Christians simply leave it to all the other Christians to get the work of the kingdom done?

Too many!

Ministry is crucial for spiritual growth. Our Lord has gifted us and commanded us to serve and give, not only because so many people need what we could do for them, but because a spiritual ministry of some kind brings about spiritual growth.

The Dead Sea is dead because it has water flowing into it but not out of it. So the water stagnates and does not support life. No fish swim in the Dead Sea. No seaweed and plant life exist there. No teeming world of living things makes up a normal ecosystem, as we see in living lakes. All because the Dead Sea only takes; it never gives.

Water without an outlet stagnates, whether it is the stinking water left rotting in the plugged-up eaves on a house, or the salty, oily water of the Dead Sea. The same thing is true of the Christian life. If we do not have sufficient information, worship, nurture, and instruction flowing into the Christian life and sufficient ministry flowing out, the Christian begins to stagnate.

That is why a chapter on "ministry" is crucial in a book on spiritual growth. There are three areas in which a Christian must minister. One is evangelism, another is building up other Christians, and a third is humanitarian acts toward those outside the church.

Why Must I Minister to Others?

The commands of Christ, the teaching of Scripture, and the needs around us demand that we accept the challenge of ministering to others.

The Pony Express was the Federal Express of its day. It wasn't exactly "overnight" service, but it sure was the fastest thing the West had ever seen. Skinny young horsemen rode from St. Joseph, Missouri, to Sacramento, California, in just ten days. They rode fast horses at a gallop for seventy-five to one hundred miles a day, changing horses every fifteen to twenty-five miles. All they could carry with them, besides the mail, was a bit of flour, cornmeal, bacon, and a first-aid kit.

It was a hard job and a dangerous job. Several years ago, my wife and I were vacationing in the Rocky Mountain National Park and we thought it would be fun to take one of the horseback rides that are available. We could choose a two-hour ride or a four-hour ride. We were excited. The weather was delightful. The scenery was spectacular. We opted for the four-hour ride.

We should have opted for the two-hour ride.

By the time we got to the halfway point, I knew we had made a serious mistake. Nails were beginning to poke up through the saddle seat. My legs were being molded into neat semi-circles. My neck was being whiplashed from the jerking of the horse as it deliberately chose rough ground to walk on. I thought, *Oh, no. I've got another two hours of this to go!*

By the time the ride was ended, I needed a chiropractor. It took me several days to recuperate.

It would be a torturous thing for an average person to ride a horse at a gallop for seventy-five to a hundred miles a day. A normal person couldn't do it. On top of the demands of staying on a horse that long, in winter the riders wore scant clothing to keep the weight down for the horse.

You might wonder how the company ever got anyone to take such a demanding job. It was simple. They put the following ad in the newspaper: WANTED: *Young, skinny, wiry fellows not over 18. Must be expert riders willing to risk daily. Orphans preferred.*

They never had a shortage of riders.

Perhaps the riders envisioned only the glamour of changing horses at nearly full-gallop, or of hearing the cheer of the crowd as they rode into Sacramento. But in reality it was long, hard, dangerous work. If the riding and the weather didn't get you, the Indians might.

Other jobs associated with the Pony Express, however, weren't so demanding. For example, Pony Express stations every ten to fifteen miles offered fresh horses, food, first-aid, and beds. Someone had to tend those stations by cooking the meals and keeping the horses fed, shod, and in good health. Someone in Missouri and California had to handle the mail. Someone had to build the way-stations and corrals. Others had to map out the routes the riders would take. Someone had to raise the money to get it started. It was a big undertaking. Many people had a role in getting the mail through.

Serving Christ is much like that. It is a big job. Some of us have the hard, dangerous trail work. Some of us have the boring work of tending the way-station. Others have the demanding task of raising the money, while still others have the technical task of mapping out and building routes to take and estimating how much time all segments of the operation will take.

God doesn't ask the person gifted to raise money to ride the horses. He doesn't ask the technical-minded person to shoe the horses. He doesn't ask the detail-oriented clerk to cook the meals. Each gift corresponds to a job. All of us have to do our part if the work of God is to be done.

Why I Need to Know This

I need to know this so that I will have the proper knowledge and motivation to become involved in ministry. This is essential not only for the sake of others, but because I will not grow spiritually to the degree I should unless I am ministering to others.

We were created by God, not just to worship Him, not just to grow in inner character, not just to enjoy each other's fellowship, but also to *do* something for Him. We have a purpose. There is a job to do, and we are responsible to help do it.

Dietrich Bonhoeffer, a German pastor who died for his faith in World War II, once said that when Christ calls us to Himself, He bids us come and die. That cannot be disputed. Romans 12:1 says, "I beseech you therefore, brethren, by the mercies of God, that you present your bodies a living sacrifice, holy, acceptable to God, which is your reasonable service." Such a verse leaves no doubt that when God calls us to Himself, He does not call us to idleness or mere comfort. Laziness is not in the list of the fruit of the Spirit (Galatians 5:22–23). When we became Christians the blood of Christ cleansed our conscience, according to Hebrews 9:14, in order for us to "serve the living God!" In Psalm 100:2, we are called upon to "serve the Lord with gladness."

Serving God is not for the casually interested or double-minded. He wants our ministry to Him to be a priority, not a pastime. He doesn't want part-time workers. Nor is there any such thing as spiritual unemployment or retirement with God.

How Does Ministry Stimulate Spiritual Growth?

Outreach stimulates spiritual growth by stretching the Christian beyond his present level and bringing about learning, maturation, and fulfillment.

A debate has raged for years, as the media of television, music, and movies have been in a moral mudslide, as to whether the media reflect moral and cultural degeneration or whether they cause it. The debate has always seemed like a bogus one to me, because it seemed so obvious that the media both reflect moral and cultural degeneration and encourage it. Much of the programming on television today would not have been accepted by the American public thirty years ago, so surely the values of the public have changed and the media reflect that change. However, television and movies helped change much of it by exposing us to lower and lower standards so that we gradually accepted them.

Just as that principle is true in the negative example of the media, so it is true in the positive example of spiritual growth. Ministry to others both reflects and encourages spiritual growth.

It reflects spiritual growth in that a person must first accept the challenge to get involved. For example, a new Christian might hold his nose and plunge into the world of teaching four- and five-year-old children at church, not really knowing a whole lot, but figuring that he could keep ahead of someone who can't even read. So, it takes a certain amount of faith and spiritual growth to be willing to do anything.

However, once he gets involved, he discovers that there are questions that four- and five-year-olds ask that he does not know the answer to. (A five-year-old once asked me, "If the devil causes so many problems, why doesn't God just kill the devil?" It sent me scrambling!) Most of the really hard, unanswerable questions about life and Christianity are asked by children before they are six years old. So, the newer Christian is stretched beyond his knowledge and understanding, so he prepares an answer for the next time. He grows in knowledge and understanding because he first got involved in ministry.

A Christian grows in knowledge and understanding when he becomes involved in ministry. Ministry encourages us to grow in other ways. For example, if you open your home to host activities for the junior high youth group from the church, you may find them looking to you as a model of Christian behavior. Perhaps one of them says, "Hey, Mrs. Smith, it's cool of you to have us in your home. You're always smiling and good to us. Thank you!" Somewhere down in the inner recesses of your heart, you know that the teenage girl saw more than was really there. But you want what she thought she saw to really be there. So you commit to becoming a more faithful and loving Christian. Your commitment to do something simple, like open your home to an activity, spurred greater spiritual growth.

As a pastor, I can give abundant testimony to the fact that ministry to others creates ministry in me. For example, I have found it very difficult to sustain the level of discipline in studying the Bible that I ought to have unless I am studying to preach, teach, or write. I find it easier to tolerate spiritual laziness or carelessness when I am not preaching, teaching, or writing. When I have to minister to others, the Holy Spirit seems to have greater sway over me. I think, *How can I say or write "that" if I am not living it?* I find I must repent more readily and more completely in order to maintain my spiritual focus, intensity, and integrity when I am ministering. In this way, too, my ministry to others encourages spiritual growth in me.

Perhaps you can identify with these examples even though you may not be a pastor. If you have trouble studying the Bible as you ought on your own, you can teach children, get involved in a Bible study, or write a devotional thought for your Sunday school's newsletter.

If you help find temporary places for homeless people to stay, the experience might have you searching the Scriptures for answers to homelessness or for answers to the questions they ask.

Regardless of what the ministry, it takes a certain level of spiritual growth to get involved in it, and then the ministry stimulates greater spiritual growth. In this way, ministry both reflects and encourages spiritual growth.

For What Ministries Is the Christian Responsible?

The Christian is responsible for evangelism, edification, and humanitarianism.

When it comes to ministering to others, every Christian has three jobs: He is responsible to evangelize, to use his spiritual gift to build up other Christians (edification), and to help the disadvantaged who cannot help themselves (humanitarianism).

We are to evangelize. In a "Peanuts" cartoon, Charlie Brown trots down the street from house to house telling everyone about the Great Pumpkin—that it will appear on Halloween night to give gifts to those who see it. Charlie's friend, Linus, is standing on the other side of the street watching him. Lucy comes up and asks Linus what he is doing. He explains that he is watching Charlie Brown tell others about the Great Pumpkin. Lucy asks why Linus isn't over there with Charlie Brown helping him tell others about the Great Pumpkin. Linus says, "I'm a semi-evange-list."

Many of us Christians are "semi-evangelists," watching other Christians tell the unsaved about Jesus while we stand, as it were, on the other side of the street. However, if we are to be biblical Christians, and if we are to have the benefit of growing spiritually as a result of ministering to others, we must get on the same side of the street as Charlie Brown, and begin evangelizing ourselves.

In Matthew 28:19–20 we read, "Go therefore and make disciples of all the nations, baptizing them in the name of the Father and of the Son and of the Holy Spirit, teaching them to observe all things that I have commanded you." This passage is called the Great Commission. Each of us is responsible to determine what we can do to help fulfill the Great Commission. We cannot do everything, but as each of us does his part, the whole body of Christ can accomplish what God wants accomplished in spreading the message of the gospel to the ends of the earth.

Some people argue that this command was given only to Jesus' disciples. However, it is impossible for Jesus' disciples to have reached the whole world by themselves. The only possible way the command can be fulfilled is by a ripple effect. As each person who is reached attempts to reach others in his world, the gospel is spread in ever-widening circles.

Telling others about the gospel is something that most Christians have a very difficult time doing. We fear what other people will think about us if they know we are Christians. Probably most of us have been embarrassed at one time or another be-

Fear of many kinds hinders us from sharing the gospel.

cause it didn't seem to be socially acceptable to be a Christian. One time early in my ministry I lied to a person who was cutting my hair when she asked what I did for a living. I felt so awkward, so out of place in the barber shop when she asked me so that others could hear my answer. Embarrassed to reveal the truth, I told her I was a landscape architect. I later called her back, confessed my lie to her, and asked her to forgive me, which she graciously did. But I lied because it seemed very uncool in that very secular setting to admit I was a Christian. That is what fear can do.

Another reason we often don't share the gospel is fear of rejection, or just the weariness of rejection, which I think is different from just fear or embarrassment. I have shared my faith many, many times when I was not embarrassed, only to have the other person begin to act as though I had leprosy. When that happens often enough, a built-in resistance can grow if we let it. Many times I have been chatting amiably with a seatmate on an airplane when the other person asks me what I do for a living. I say, "I am a minister," to which the other person says, "Oh . . . ," then mentions that he or she has a cousin who is religious. Then my seatmate unfolds the newspaper and begins reading. Conversation over. It has happened a hundred times in a multitude of different ways. And it can make you reluctant to try to witness if you're not careful.

Sometimes people don't witness because they feel they don't know enough. However, if someone knows enough to have become a Christian, he knows enough to tell someone else as much as he knows. It is helpful to know the Bible well and to be aware of common objections to Christianity. But the bottom line is that we can always tell people what we understand and what happened to us.

We can always tell others about our own experience of salvation.

That being the case, we must discipline ourselves to evangelize. Colossians 4:5–6 says, "Be wise in the way you act toward outsiders; make the most of every opportunity. Let your conversation be always full of grace, seasoned with salt, so that you may know how to answer everyone" (NIV). We must have determined ahead of time our role in the Great Commission. We must make the most of opportunities we have with the unchurched, which means we must be geared for and on the lookout for opportunities. If the normal course of our lives does not put us in contact with non-Christians we must pray for and create ways to have contact with them. We can manifest the love of Christ to the non-Christians we come in contact with in nonverbal ways by being kind, friendly, honest, courteous, etc. A big part of life is behaving in such a way toward everyone so that if they find out we are a Christian, it will make a good impression on them. We must even drive in such a way that if other drivers on the road find out we are a Christian, our driving will make a good impression on them.

Although important, these nonverbal things are not enough. Sooner or later, we must actually share the message of the gospel with others or create opportunities for them to be exposed to the gospel through a third means (by inviting them to a special meeting, or giving them a book, or recommending to them an evangelistic broadcast).

When a commitment to evangelism resides in our heart, the Lord will lead us to His ways to fulfill that commitment.

We are to edify one another. The apostle Paul in Ephesians 4:11–12 explains that we are to minister to one another to build each other to maturity in Christ: "And He Himself gave some to be apostles, some prophets, some evangelists, and some pastors and teachers, for the equipping of the saints for the work of ministry, for the [building up] of the body of Christ."

Many of us don't get involved ministering to one another because we don't realize we are gifted by God for that purpose. But 1 Peter 4:10 applies to us: "As each one has received a gift, minister it to one another." We don't realize that other people need us.

Perhaps we haven't fully understood that God expects us to minister to others. Perhaps we haven't admitted that we are so busy with other things that we don't want to know that God expects us to minister to others.

But He does.

God expects us to minister to others. Bud Wilkinson, former coach of the Oklahoma Sooners, once was asked if he thought football was a good influence on Americans to be physically fit. "Not at all," he answered. "In football, you have 60,000 fans in the stands in desperate need of exercise, watching twenty-two players on the field in desperate need of rest."

How like the church! Too many people watch the few people in desperate need of rest.

For another example, imagine you are watching a football game with the coaches and players huddled on the sidelines just before the game begins. Soon the huddle breaks with a simultaneous "Rah!" at which the coaches run out on the field to play and the players stay on the sidelines and cheer.

It's a ridiculous image, but not far from what happens each week in the local church. The Ephesians passage shows us that the pastor and teachers are to equip the saints for the work of the ministry, not to do all the work of the ministry themselves. The pastor and teachers are like coaches, training and equipping laypersons to be the players. When laypersons do not involve themselves in ministry, it is like the football players staying on the sidelines while the coaches go out and try to play all the positions. It doesn't work.

If you are a Christian, you are supposed to be doing something for the benefit of other Christians. I know you are busy. I know you may not feel equipped. I know you may think that others are better able to serve than you. None of that changes the Bible. You are supposed to be doing something.

"What?" you ask. Well, you can pick from the list in Romans 12:4–8:

- prophecy (proclaiming the word of God)
- service (helping others succeed at what they feel called to do)
- teaching (helping others understand the Bible and spiritual truth)
- exhortation (motivating others to do what they should)
- giving (supporting ministries financially)
- leading (helping give vision and direction to ministry)
- mercy (showing kindness and helping the needy)

This is probably not intended to be a complete list, but a sample list of the kinds of things God enables believers to do. If you see something that needs to be done and you think you can, then very likely you are gifted in that area. Go for it. Serve others. We all need you. Come off the sidelines and into the game. The ministry of the church will not be complete without you, and your own spiritual growth will not be developed without your involvement.

We are to be involved in humanitarianism. No matter how much money we give, we cannot help everyone. Even Jesus admitted that the poor would always be with us (Matthew 26:11). Nevertheless, we must share with the less fortunate around us from our own resources.

> **Though we cannot do everything, we must do something.**

No matter how much time we have, we cannot help everyone. I have met some needy people who were a full-time job just by themselves. When I started trying to help them, it was like stepping into a black hole. They consumed my whole life. Obviously, we cannot do that with everyone, and we cannot do it at all if we have a large family depending on us.

Helping the disadvantaged requires thinking and praying about your role and not getting in over your head. However, most people not only fear getting in over their heads, they fear getting in over their toenails. They conclude, erroneously, that since they cannot help everyone, they don't have to help anyone. Not true. While some of us will be more involved in helping the disadvantaged than others, all of us must do something. We must all pray to ask God what He wants us to do, and then be faithful to that.

The apostle James writes, "If a brother or sister is naked and destitute of daily food, and one of you says to them, 'Depart in peace, be warmed and filled,' but you do not give them the things which are needed for the body, what does it profit?" (James 2:15–16).

James 1:27 says, "This is pure and undefiled religion in the sight of our God and Father, to visit orphans and widows in their distress" (NASB). We are to care for those less fortunate than ourselves, and who cannot take care of themselves.

There are no loopholes here, only responsibilities. We may not be able to help everyone, but we must help some. They need it, and we need it. We will not grow spiritually unless we are faithful in this area of obedience to Christ.

These and many other tasks we as Christians are supposed to do. If we are not sharing our faith, serving with our gifts, and exercising our responsibilities, we are indicating inadequate spiritual growth. It is a sign that we have not accepted the lordship of Christ in certain matters of service and that we are willing to ignore Christ's commands. It is evidence that we have not yet grown spiritually.

How Do We Remain Motivated for the Sacrifice of Ministry?

We remain motivated for the sacrifice of outreach by remembering it is an obligation because of what Christ and others have done for us.

In many cases, ministry to others is a matter of discipline. We do it not always because it is rewarding, but because a job needs to be done and God has called us to do it.

For example, friends often ask me how I enjoy pastoring. Well, I enjoy parts of it, and parts of it I don't like at all. I like Sunday morning services, special gatherings where there is food, men's re-treats, and church golf tournaments. But I don't like funerals, hospital crises, and counseling people whose spouse has just left. But those are part of the job. You take the bitter with the sweet.

In pastoring, I find myself doing some things simply because they go with the ministry and I am responsible. While much of it isn't fun, I find it very rewarding on two levels. One, I am able to help people who urgently need it. And two, I have been faithful to God in discharging my duty to Him and the gift He has given me. That means more and more to me the older I get. It is deeply satisfying to lay my head on my pillow at night knowing that that day, as much as I knew how, I did what God wanted me to do.

It is satisfying to know that you did what God wanted you to do.

The same is true for all of us who minister. Certainly, we should take overall satisfaction from it. But one of the fundamental reasons we minister is because we have been gifted by God and commanded by Him to do so.

John Newton, the author of "Amazing Grace," possibly the best known and loved hymn ever written, once wrote:

> If two angels were to receive at the same moment a commission from God, one to go down and rule earth's grandest empire, the other to go and sweep the streets of its meanest village, it would be a matter of entire indifference to each which service fell to his lot, the post of ruler or the post of scavenger; for the joy of the angels lies only in obedience to God's will (quoted in E. M. Bound's book, *The Essentials of Prayer*, 19).

If we had the same eternal perspective on this life, we would be more willing to serve the Lord by serving others. Having said all that, let me add that there are times when we can take time off from ministry. It has not been uncommon in my pastoral experience that people would come to our church burned to a frazzle from overcommitment, usually in a smaller church where there were not enough committed people to go around. All these wornout workers wanted to do was hide. That's fine—for a while. We all need recovery times. But when we have recovered, we need to regroup and reapply ourselves to ministry.

A second motive for ministry is gratitude to God and others for what they have done for us. When I think of what people have sacrificed to minister to me; when I reflect upon the faith-fulness of God in bringing to me just what I needed when I needed it; when I contemplate how I would have struggled if people had not ministered to me so faithfully; and when I imagine how others will struggle if I don't minister to them, I find great inspiration and unexpected emotional reserve for ministry.

Donald Whitney in his book, *Spiritual Disciplines for the Christian Life*, has said it as well as I have ever heard it:

> Do you remember what it is like not to know Christ, to be without God and without hope? Do you remember what it is like to be guilty before God and unforgiven? Do you remember what it is like to have offended God and to have His anger burning toward you? Do you remember what it is like to be only a heartbeat away from hell? Now do you remember what it is like to see Jesus Christ with the eyes of faith and to understand for the first time who He really is and what He has done by His death and resurrection? Do you remember what it was like to experience forgiveness and deliverance from judgment and hell? Do you remember what it was first like to have the assurance of Heaven and eternal life? When the fire of service to God grows cold, consider what great things the Lord has done for you.
>
> He has never done anything greater for anyone, nor could He do anything greater for you, than bring you to Himself. Suppose He put ten million dollars into your bank account every morning for the rest of your life, but He didn't save you? Suppose He gave you the most beautiful body and face of anyone who ever lived, a body that never aged for a thousand years, but then at death He shut you out of heaven and into hell for eternity? What has God ever given anyone that could compare with the salvation He has given you as a believer? Do you see that there is nothing God could ever do for you or give to you greater than the gift of Himself? If we cannot be grateful servants of Him who is everything and in whom we have everything, what will make us grateful? (112–113).

Certainly, this point is well taken. However, some might easily say "no" to several of these questions simply because they grew up in a Christian home and cannot remember when they did not believe in Jesus and have the assurance of forgiveness of sin and hope of heaven. In those cases, the person can try to imagine what it would be like if they did not have those hopes and assurances.

Conclusion

Whether we remember it from our pre-Christian days, or whether we must imagine it, the burden of bearing our own sin is incomprehensible. The weight of hopelessness after death is immeasurable. The depth of meaninglessness in this life is unfathomable. There is no way to calculate the loss of not having Christ—or the gain of having Him.

What would you do if you had not heard of Him? How would you cope? What would your life be like? What are you willing to give of time, talents, and treasure to get the message of truth and hope to others that gives such peace to you?

Speed Bump!

Slow down to be sure you've gotten the main points of this chapter.

Q1. Why must I minister to others?

A1. The commands of Christ, the teaching of Scripture, and the needs around us demand that we *accept* the challenge of ministering to others.

Q2. How does ministry stimulate spiritual growth?

A2. Outreach stimulates spiritual growth by *stretching* the Christian beyond his present level and bringing about learning, maturation, and fulfillment.

Q3. For what ministries is the Christian responsible?

A3. The Christian is *responsible* for evangelism, edification, and humanitarianism.

Q4. How do we remain motivated for the sacrifice of ministry?

A4. We remain motivated for the sacrifice of outreach by remembering it is an *obligation* because of what Christ and others have done for us.

Fill in the Blank

$\mathcal{Q}$uestion
$\mathcal{A}$nswer

Q1. Why must I minister to others?

A1. The commands of Christ, the teaching of Scripture and the needs around us demand that we _____ the challenge of ministering to others.

Q2. How does ministry stimulate spiritual growth?

A2. Outreach stimulates spiritual growth by _____ the Christian beyond his present level and bringing about learning, maturation, and fulfillment.

Q3. For what ministries is the Christian responsible?

A3. The Christian is _____ for evangelism, edification, and humanitarianism.

Q4. How do we remain motivated for the sacrifice of ministry?

A4. We remain motivated for the sacrifice of outreach by remembering it is an _____ because of what Christ and others have done for us.

For Further Thought and Discussion

1. Have you ever accepted the obligation you have as a Christian to minister to others? How do you think you could serve others?

2. Have you ever had an experience, perhaps not associated with the church, in which you grew in your ability or as a person because you agreed to do something? Explain.

3. Of the three sets of responsibilities—evangelism, edification, and humanitarianism—which one do you gravitate toward most naturally? What do you think that might tell you about how you should use your time and gifts? What should you do to not neglect the other areas?

4. What do you think you would miss the most if you had never become a Christian? What are you most grateful for in having become a Christian? How can those motivate you to share the gospel with others?

What If I Don't Believe?

If I don't believe that I have an obligation to minister to others, I probably will not do so. It is hard enough to do when I feel the obligation, let alone if I didn't feel it. By not ministering to others, I won't grow. I will not be as fulfilled as a Christian as I would otherwise be, nor be as valuable to the body of Christ as I could be.

For Further Study

1. Scripture

- Matthew 28:19–20
- Romans 12:4–8
- Galatians 6:10
- Ephesians 4:11–12
- Colossians 4:5–6
- 1 Peter 4:10

2. Books

Gentle Persuasion, Joseph Aldrich
Unleashing the Church, Frank Tillapaugh

10

How Do Inward Spiritual Disciplines Help Me Grow Spiritually?

The Christian life has been described as a battle to be fought, a race to be run, and a building to be constructed. In each of these cases, certain disciplines must be followed if the goal is to be reached.

For example, boot camp for a soldier is one of the most demanding experiences in life. James Herriot, the beloved Scottish veterinarian and storyteller, described his experience just before World War II in his book, *All Things Wise and Wonderful*:

> "Move!" bawled the drill corporal. "Come on, speed it up!" He sprinted effortlessly to the rear of the gasping, panting column of men and urged us on from there.
>
> I was somewhere in the middle, jog-trotting laboriously with the rest and wondering how much longer I could keep going. And as my ribs heaved agonizingly and my leg muscles protested I tried to work out just how many miles we had run.

After running what Herriot had thought was a ridiculous, near-impossible distance, he reeled through the streets of London only to hear the corporal announce the next level of pain:

> "Awright lads," he had cried, smiling over the fifty new airmen. "We're just going to trot round to the park, so follow me. Le-eft turn! At the double, qui-ick march! 'eft-ight, 'eft-'ight, 'eft-ight!"

They ran for a long, long time, with never a sign of a park anywhere. Finally, the corporal chirped from the rear that they were almost there, and sure enough, after rounding a corner, they finally caught sight of the park. Thinking that they had neared the end of their agonizing journey, a sense of relief swept through the corps. Herriot judged that he had just enough strength to make it through the gates of the park, but no more, because his legs were beginning to seize up. As they passed through the gate, the corporal shouted for them to run around the track that circled the outside of the park. A storm of protest rose from the recruits, but was quickly subdued by a furious scowl and threats of how much worse things would get if they didn't obey immediately. So around the track they went. After they had done the impossible—run around the track after getting to the park which they had thought they couldn't get to—the corporal sounded again:

"Round again, lads!" the corporal yelled, and as we stared at him aghast he smiled affectionately. "You think this is tough? Wait till they get hold of you at ITW. I'm just kinda breakin' you in gently. You'll thank me for this later. Right, at the double! One-two, one-two!"

Bitter thoughts assailed me as I lurched forward once more. Another round of the park would kill me—there was not a shadow of a doubt about that. You left a loving wife and a happy home to serve king and country and this was how they treated you. It wasn't fair (1–2).

Not only is the physical punishment almost beyond endurance, other things about military life take getting used to. My Uncle Don used to tell the story of when he was in the Army at Ft. Leonard Wood, Missouri. They were bivouacking for three weeks in the wilderness under extremely demanding conditions, marching endlessly, engaging in military maneuvers, and trying to keep their feet and rifles clean. The food was terrible! The first week, when the soldiers got their first meal, they noticed bugs in the food. But they had been pushed so hard, and they were so tired and hungry, they just picked them out and ate the food anyway. During the second week, bugs still speckled the food, but the soldiers were even more tired and hungry, so they just ate the food with the bugs in it. By the third week there were still bugs in the food, but the men were more tired and hungrier than ever, so they poked around on the ground for additional bugs to throw in the food to supplement it!

The point is that certain disciplines and training must be completed or one does not make a good soldier, and a bad soldier is likely to get killed in action or get other people killed. Discipline is the main characteristic of good soldiers. They must be physically fit, they must know their weapons and how to use them, they must understand warfare, and they must be trained to obey orders instantly. All this takes discipline unimaginable to anyone who hasn't gone through it.

Discipline also underlies athletics. Olympic athletes must often rise early in the morning to practice, then go to school, then practice some more. An Olympic athlete may practice eight to twelve hours a day for four to six years or more just to be able to do one fairly simple thing better than anyone else has ever done it.

The same is true with constructing a building. I lived in Atlanta during its boom years when the remarkable ATT building was being constructed. A year was spent getting the foundation dug, prepared, and poured. It took only another year to finish the entire fifty-story building. A building of that size must be constructed with scrupulous attention to detail and the laws of physics. You cannot slap something like that together without risking the whole thing coming down in a heap due to gravity, earthquake, or storm.

Just as the military, athletics, and construction must be characterized by great discipline, so must the Christian life be. But discipline is really the price for freedom. Lack of discipline enslaves one to weakness and ignorance. In discussing spiritual disciplines, we are not talking about things that will limit us, but about the things necessary to get what we want out of our spiritual relationship with God and others.

In this chapter we learn that . . .

1. Meditation allows the Holy Spirit to renew the mind and provide deep illumination of spiritual truth.
2. Prayer is conversation with God which allows for requests to be made, communion to be experienced, and reconciliation to the will of God to be realized.
3. Fasting allows a high level of concentration and physical deprivation which heightens spiritual sensitivity.

Hours of calisthenics, marching, and military maneuvers give the soldier the freedom to win in battle. Hours of repetition and practice equip the athlete with the impetus to win his race. Scrupulous attention to detail allows the architect the freedom to construct great buildings that benefit humanity in both form and function.

So it is with spiritual disciplines. Faithfulness to exercise, repetition, and scrupulous attention to detail bestow upon the Christian the freedom to understand God and spiritual truth, the strength to overcome bad habits, the vision to guide his life in a satisfying direction, the insight to discern the will of God, and the endurance to keep going in the tough times.

Everyone is a slave to something and free *from* something. One can practice the spiritual disciplines and be free to experience the insight and power he wants in the Christian life, or he can be free from the spiritual disciplines and be a slave to frustration and confusion.

In the spirit of freedom and power, not the spirit of limitation and drudgery, we introduce our study of the spiritual disciplines. Spiritual disciplines open the door to spiritual liberation. Of course, everything worthwhile has its price. A deep, meaningful, spiritual walk with God and other Christians is costly.

In our study of the spiritual disciplines, we will look at three basic types. The inward disciplines cultivate the inner spiritual life. The outward disciplines govern individual activities we can pursue to encourage spiritual growth, and in the corporate disciplines we join other Christians in mutual ministry for spiritual growth.

In this chapter, we begin by looking at three inward disciplines.

What Is the Role of Meditation in Spiritual Growth?

Meditation allows the Holy Spirit to renew the mind and provide deep illumination of spiritual truth.

In a phrase often quoted, G. K. Chesterton, a deceased English wit, once said, "Christianity has not so much been tried and found wanting, as it has been found difficult and left untried." Yes, Christianity is difficult. But no matter how hard it is to be obedient to Christ, disobedience is harder. We hear often of the high cost of discipleship, but the price of non-discipleship makes it pale in comparison. It exacts more from a person to go to hell than to heaven, even before he gets there.

The Book of Proverbs eloquently records the exorbitant cost of sin and the benefits of righteousness. It drives home the reality of the "easy yoke" which Jesus spoke about in Matthew 11:29–30: "Take my yoke upon you and learn from Me, for I am gentle and lowly in heart, and you will find rest for your souls. For My yoke is easy and My burden is light."

In his book, *The Spirit of the Disciplines,* Dallas Willard has written,

> To depart from righteousness is to choose a life of crushing burdens, failures, and disappointments, a life caught in the toils of endless problems that are never resolved. Here is the source of that unending soap opera, that sometimes horror show known as normal human life. The "cost of discipleship," though it may take all we have, is small when compared to the lot of those who don't accept Christ's invitation to be part of his company in The Way of life (2).

In order to avoid the unnecessary costs of un-discipleship, we must know the Bible so well that we think of its truths and apply them in life's situations. In order to know the Bible that well, we must constantly be reviewing it in our mind. By this constant or frequent review, we practice a key spiritual discipline, meditation.

Why I Need to Know This

I need to know this so that I will understand the benefits of meditating, praying, and fasting. Unless I understand how important they are, I am liable to undervalue them. But if I exercise these spiritual disciplines, I can free myself to ascend to a higher plane of spiritual walk.

Biblical meditation is not the meditation often associated with transcendental meditation, eastern religions, yoga, relaxation/stress-reduction therapy, or the New Age Movement. Because meditation is common in these non-Christian groups, many Christians are initially uncomfortable with the subject. However, the words *meditate* and *meditation* occur many times in the Bible, and many giants of the faith, especially David, practiced meditation as part of their everyday life.

By far the most common usage is to meditate on the Scriptures or on an attribute or work of God. Understood biblically, to meditate does not mean to "let one's mind go blank" and think about *nothing*, as is common in other religions, but rather to meditate upon *something:* to mull over the truth of Scripture, praying and searching for new truths, deeper appreciation for truths already observed, and doing what we know and understand. Meditation has been defined as "deep thinking on the truths and spiritual realities revealed in Scripture for the purposes of understanding, application, and prayer" (*Spiritual Disciplines for the Christian Life,* Donald Whitney, 44).

Joshua 1:8 says, "This Book of the Law shall not depart from your mouth, but you shall meditate in it day and night, that you may observe to do according to all that is written in it. For then you will make your way prosperous, and then you will have good success."

This passage includes a powerful promise for prosperity and success. However, there is no magic in memorizing and meditating on Scripture. The prosperity and success come when we have become so familiar with the Scripture through meditation that we are careful to *do* all that our increased understanding suggests we do. Puritan pastor Thomas Watson once wrote, "The reason we come away so cold from reading the word is, because we do not warm ourselves at the fire of meditation" (*Puritan Sermons,* Vol. II, 62). As we meditate, the Lord gives us increased insight. As we act on our increased insight, we enjoy spiritual prosperity and success.

Psalm 1:1–3 amplifies the promises. When one delights in the law and meditates in it day and night, he is fruitful, he does not wither, and he prospers. Someone once said, "He thrives best who meditates most." These verses would seem to support that idea. In Psalm 119:98–99, David said that he was wiser than all his enemies and had more insight than all his teachers because he meditated on God's statutes.

> "He thrives best who meditates most."

Meditation is a more critical discipline today than it has ever been, in my opinion, because the electronic media and the furious pace of modern life leave little space for "down time." Many people turn the TV on first thing in the morning to catch the news, listen to radio all day when working, listen to music when driving the car, and turn on the TV after work to catch the news again, leaving it on until bedtime. There is no time when the mind can think about thoughts that are not being artificially injected into it.

Since we become like what we think about, we adopt the world's knowledge, habits, values, behavior, perspective, likes, and dislikes. If we want to have the *Word's* habits, values, behavior, perspective, likes, and dislikes, we must allow our mind to dwell on the truth of Scripture. That can only happen as we stop the flow of the artificial input and meditate upon God's Word.

If we watch TV regularly, listen to worldly music frequently, read secular magazines, work hard at our jobs, and sense that God is obscure, the Christian life hard, heaven far away, and circumstances overwhelming—if we feel on Sunday morning that life ought to be more than it is, but we fall back into our trap on Monday morning—we shouldn't be surprised. The Bible does not yield its treasures so easily. The Holy Spirit does not deeply reward so superficial a relationship. The Lord does not bless carelessness, mediocrity, ignorance, or busyness.

The Lord does not bless carelessness, mediocrity, ignorance, or busyness.

The electric light bulb transformed life all over the world. It was invented by Thomas Edison, a genius who has many revolutionary inventions to his credit. Someone once asked him how he came up with the idea for the light bulb and figured out how to make it work. He replied, "By thinking about it all the time."

If we love something enough, it will eventually tell us its secrets. How true this is of the Bible. If we will simply focus on it to the extent that the Bible tells us we should, it will begin to tell us secrets we would never have known otherwise.

It is impossible to learn how to meditate by reading a book, just as it is impossible to learn how to swim by reading a book. We learn to meditate by meditating. And like most skills, we usually begin doing it poorly, clumsily. But as we keep doing it, the clumsiness smooths out, the shallowness deepens, and that which felt unnatural begins feeling natural.

If you are to benefit from the spiritual discipline of meditating, you must do several things.

- You must commit yourself to meditation. Those who are half-hearted about it won't last long.

- You must lock passages from Scripture in your heart. Memorize those that are most meaningful to you. If you don't have any, start reading in Psalms, Proverbs, and the New Testament and underline verses that jump out at you. Then choose from among them the passages you will memorize and meditate upon. Memorization is important because meditation is only effective as we allow the words to turn over and over in our mind and are able to recall scriptural truth in the midst of life's circumstances.

You might buy a Scripture memorization curriculum. An excellent one from the Navigators can be purchased at most Christian bookstores.

- You must commit the time necessary for meditation, and it also would help to have a place of solitude, where you can meditate uninterrupted.

After you have selected a verse or passage (and I would recommend not starting with too long a passage—a verse or two is fine), then you might try the following ways to get your mind to focus on the truth of the passage so that God can begin to reveal its depths to you. Some of these ideas were adapted from Donald Whitney's book, *Spiritual Disciplines for the Christian Life*, chapter 3.

- Repeat the passage over and over, either in your mind or, if you are alone, out loud. Look for deeper meanings and insights into the passage. One helpful technique is to say the passage repeatedly, emphasizing a different word each time. For example, John 11:25:

  "*I* am the resurrection and the life."
  "I *am* the resurrection and the life."
  "I am *the* resurrection and the life."
  "I am the *resurrection* and the life."
  "I am the resurrection *and* the life."
  "I am the resurrection and *the* life."
  "I am the resurrection and the *life*."

  The purpose is not rote repetition, but by concentrating on each word to gain new and deeper understanding from the passage.

- Rewrite the passage in your own words. Or say the passage in your own words, substituting synonyms for some words, and longer explanations for others.

- Pray through the passage: "Dear Lord, thank you that you are the resurrection and the life. Thank you that you were willing to die for my sins, and that you came to life again. I am grateful that you rose again from the dead and made it possible for me to rise again from the dead. I thank you that the life you promise me is not just physical life, and not just everlasting life, but it is abundant life."

- Return to a given passage many times. Sometimes you might spend a week, meditating as often as you can on one verse or passage.

- Study the passage using a good Bible commentary to make sure you understand it. Ask yourself continually, "What does this passage mean to me?"

- Be obedient to any new insights you receive. Light received brings more light. Light rejected recedes into darkness.

- Like Thomas Edison and his light bulb, think about your passage whenever your mind does not have to be occupied on other matters.

Dallas Willard wrote, in *The Spirit of the Disciplines:*

Memorization and meditation upon Scripture can transform both the inner and outer life.

As a pastor, teacher, and counselor I have repeatedly seen the transformation of inner and outer life that comes simply from memorization and meditation upon Scripture. Personally, I would never undertake to pastor a church or guide a program of Christian education that did not involve a continuous program of memorization of the choicest passages of Scripture for people of all ages (150).

So, too, we each ought to undertake this discipline for ourselves.

Romans 12:1–2 says,

I beseech you, therefore, brethren, by the mercies of God, that you present your bodies a living sacrifice, holy, acceptable to God, which is your reasonable service. And do not be conformed to this world, but be transformed by the renewing of your mind, that you may prove what is that good and acceptable and perfect will of God.

The passage tells us that if we would be living demonstrations of the truth that God's will is good and acceptable and perfect, then we must have our mind renewed. What more effective way to have our mind renewed than to memorize and meditate upon Scripture?

What Is the Role of Prayer in Spiritual Growth?

Prayer is conversation with God which allows for requests to be made, communion to be experienced, and reconciliation to the will of God to be realized.

For some people prayer is a foreign activity, a disagreeable idea. Wimps or sissies pray, but not people who stand on their own two feet. After all, God helps those who help themselves. In this vein, Bill Hybels, in his book, *Too Busy Not to Pray* has written:

Prayer is an unnatural activity.

From birth we have been learning the rules of self-reliance as we strain and struggle to achieve self-sufficiency. Prayer flies in the face of those deep-seated values. It is an assault on human autonomy, an indictment of independent living. To people in the fast lane, determined to make it on their own, prayer is an embarrassing interruption (7).

Yet there are other reasons why people don't pray. They may not understand how to pray. They may stay too busy to pray. They may have tried praying, didn't get the results they thought the Bible promised, and stopped. Others feel no need to pray. They don't see that their lives go better when they do pray, or worse when they don't. So prayer seems irrelevant.

So why should we pray? Why would we make prayer a spiritual discipline?

While this is not a book on why to pray or how to pray, we need to look at these issues before we talk about the discipline of prayer.

We should pray because Jesus expects us to. In Matthew 6, one of the great "prayer" chapters in the Bible, Jesus is preaching one of His three great sermons in the Bible, the Sermon on the Mount, a penetrating discourse on godly living. In it He says,

- "And when you pray . . ." (v. 5)

- "But you, when you pray . . ." (v. 6)

- "But when you pray . . ." (v. 7)

- "In this manner, therefore, pray . . ." (v. 9).

Jesus expects us to pray.

He goes on in Luke 11,

- "When you pray, say . . ." (v. 2)

- "And I say to you, ask . . . , seek . . . , knock . . ." (v. 9).

And in Luke 18:1, we read, "Then He spoke a parable to them, that men always ought to pray and not lose heart."

So we can have little doubt that Jesus, who is God, wants and expects us to pray.

Be aware of the presence of God at all times. This conclusion is supported by other passages of Scripture that instruct and command us to pray. In 1 Thessalonians 5:17 we read "Pray without ceasing" and in Colossians 4:2, "Devote yourselves to prayer" (NIV). If we are devoted to golf, we spend the money and take the time required to play golf. If we are devoted to classical music, we invest the money and time to purchase and listen to classical music, perhaps even buying season tickets to the symphony. If we are devoted to prayer, we will make the effort and take the time needed to pray.

To "pray without ceasing" does not mean that we do nothing except pray, but rather that we do nothing without praying. We will be consciously aware of the presence of God at all times, and mentally pray and commune with Him as we go about our daily tasks.

So, the first reason we pray is because Jesus expects us to and the Bible instructs and commands us to.

We should pray because God wants us to. While this is very similar to the first reason, it emphasizes why Jesus expects us to pray and the Bible commands us to pray. God wants us to pray. In Luke 18:2–5, Jesus tells the story of a widow who was in trouble and went to a judge to get justice. The judge was not a man of high integrity, but he finally granted the woman's request because she came to him so often that he saw she was going to wear him out. The point is made, then, that if the "unjust judge" was willing to grant the woman's request, how much more God, who is just, is willing to grant our requests.

We think that God is off in a corner of the universe somewhere doing big things, or trying to keep nuclear war from breaking out, or containing some evil angel rebellion, and that He doesn't have time or interest for our petty matters. That could not be further from the truth. An omniscient and omnipotent God has no trouble running the universe and still having time for us. We are the reason everything exists in the first place. We are not an afterthought or secondary interest for God. We are "it." The Bible says we are the "apple of God's eye." Nothing is more important than we are. He wants us to pray.

We should pray because prayer can deepen our understanding of and establish our walk with God. We cannot have a deep, meaningful relationship with anyone without spending time with that person. The same is true with God. Meditating on His Word and praying to Him are the primary ways we deepen our walk with God.

Of course, this is harder with God, because He isn't visible. Nevertheless, if we believe that He is "there," then our relationship becomes richer and fuller as we spend time with Him in prayer and meditation.

We see a sublime example of prayer, meditation, and deepening relationship with God happen before our eyes in Psalm 63:1–6, as David prayed:

> O GOD, Thou art my God;/I shall seek Thee earnestly;/My soul thirsts for Thee,/my flesh yearns for Thee,/In a dry and weary land where there is no water./Thus I have beheld Thee in the sanctuary,/To see Thy power and Thy glory./Because Thy lovingkindness is better than life,/My lips will praise Thee./So I will bless Thee as long as I live;/I will lift up my hands in Thy name./My soul is satisfied as with marrow and fatness,/And my mouth offers praises with joyful lips./When I remember Thee on my bed,/I meditate on Thee in the night watches,/For Thou hast been my help,/And in the shadow of Thy wings I sing for joy (NASB).

We should pray because God answers prayer. Jesus boldly states in Matthew 7:7–8 concerning answers to prayer: "Ask, and it will be given to you; seek, and you will find; knock, and it will be opened to you. For everyone who asks receives, and he who seeks finds, and to him who knocks, it will be opened."

> Pray in all the light available to you from Scripture.

Many people have asked and not received, have sought and did not find, have knocked and it was not opened to them. As a result, they have concluded that either God does not answer prayer and this is a bogus promise, or that there is something inherently spiritually deficient about them, so for some reason, while it might work with others, it doesn't work with them.

That is the wrong conclusion, however. In looking at all the passages in Scripture about prayer, we learn of other factors to be considered. We must examine our prayers to see if we are praying in all the light and understanding available to us from the Scripture. For example, the Bible tells us of other qualifications to our prayers.

Willingly tolerating personal sin (Psalm 66:18), treating one's wife badly (1 Peter 3:7), or rejecting God's Word (Proverbs 28:9) all will hinder our prayers.

We also must pray in faith without doubting (James 1:6), in God's will (1 John 5:14), without selfish motives (James 4:3), and with persistence (Luke 18:1–8). Several of these qualifications must be more fully understood, however.

First, to pray without doubting does not mean that we must muster up the ability to believe that God absolutely will do what we ask, but rather, we believe that if He chooses, He *can*. If we must believe that God will do what we ask, then we fall into a "name it and claim it" mentality in which God will do whatever we ask if we just believe hard enough. I don't think that is the way it works.

Second, we often don't know what God's will is, so it confuses us to know how to pray in His will. However, the Scriptures can be very helpful in determining God's will in many cases. If the Bible instructs or commands us to do something or not do something, we know what God's will is in that area. So we know not to pray for anything that is contrary to the will of God. I once heard of an unmarried Christian couple who knelt down and asked God's blessing on their relationship just before they had premarital sex. They could have saved themselves some time. God was not interested in that prayer. It violated His will.

Prayer that violates God's will can bring no blessing.
A degree of common sense also can help us determine God's will. It seems a little inconsistent to ask God to bless the meal we are about to eat if the food is cholesterol-ridden, deep-fat-fried food, loaded with chemicals and preservatives and artificial color, and the drink is chemical-laden, caffeine-infested, carbonated sugar-water. If we know the food is bad for us, we can thank Him that we are not going hungry, but I don't know if it makes sense to ask Him to bless it to the nourishment of our bodies when we already know it will not be good for us.

When I have no option but to eat something that I know isn't good for me, I have sometimes prayed, with tongue only partly in cheek, "Oh, Lord, please preserve us from that which we are about to eat." To ask God's blessing on food that we know is bad for us, and that we are willingly, perhaps eagerly eating, is like the little boy who, after completing the geography exam prayed, "Dear Lord, please make Chicago the capital of Illinois!" It won't work. It's too late.

Finally, regarding our persistence in prayer, it may be helpful to speculate as to some reasons why the Lord might delay His answer for a while. I think there may be five reasons why God delays answers to prayer. (I have written about these in *30 Days to Understanding How to Live as a Christian*.)

1. It may be that the timing is not right. He intends to answer, but only after other circumstances have come together.
2. It may be He wants to clarify the request. When the answer comes, God wants us to be able to recognize it. Often we don't recognize the answer to a prayer because we did not crystallize the request in our minds.
3. He might want to create a sense of expectation and to call attention to the fact that it was He who answered, and not just good luck or natural consequences.
4. He might want to deepen our understanding of Him and His Word.
5. He might want to use the delay to draw us into a deeper relationship with Him (273–274).

When things come easily they are taken lightly. God does not want prayer to be taken lightly. Therefore, answers do not always come easily. When we fear our prayer is not being answered, and we can find no personal reason why, it may be that the answer is being delayed for one or more of the above reasons. From these passages, I believe that when we pray for something and God does not show us that we should alter or eliminate the request, we are free to ask for it until we receive it.

We learn to pray by praying. Of course, we can read books, we can study the Scriptures, and we can listen to others who pray well, thereby receiving instruction from all of them. But these things will not make pray-ers out of us. We *can* do these things but we *must* pray. If we do not know how to pray, we should pray anyway. We must risk praying badly. After all, we must start somewhere, so we just tell God that we don't know how to pray, but we want to pray, so here is our best shot. He will guide us from there.

Finally, we must make the fundamental point as it relates to this book. Prayer is a spiritual discipline. We do not pray only because we feel like it. We do not pray only when we know exactly what to pray. We do not pray whenever we think the Spirit moves us. We discipline ourselves to pray. We grab ourselves by the nape of the neck, and we pray as well as we know how. God sees the thoughts and intents of our hearts, and answers accordingly (Romans 8:26–27).

All spiritually mature people in the Bible and throughout church history have been people of prayer. Even though we may not understand all we wish we did about prayer, we do know some about prayer, and we must not let that which we do not know keep us from that which we do know. We must pray!

What Is the Role of Fasting in Spiritual Growth?

Fasting allows a high level of concentration and physical deprivation which heightens spiritual sensitivity.

It is easy to wonder why God would want us to fast. What does being hungry have to do with spiritual growth? Yet Jesus, as well as spiritual giants in the Scriptures and throughout the ages, fasted along with praying. So there must be something to it.

Certainly, fasting demonstrates an earnestness and commitment that God honors (Esther 4:16). It is so hard to go without food that we would only do it for a significant reason. By fasting, we can demonstrate to God the intensity of our spiritual longing (Nehemiah 9:1–2).

In addition, suffering (and there is, sometimes, a degree of genuine suffering for some people when they go without food) sharpens spiritual perception and obedience. We·can gain heightened spiritual living from a time of fasting, and in doing so, realize that other bread can be as important as food (Matthew 4:1–11).

The Christian poet Edna St. Vincent Millay expressed the discovery of this other "food" in her poem, "Feast":

I drank at every vine.
The last was like the first I came upon no wine
So wonderful as thirst. I gnawed at every root.
I ate of every plant. I came upon no fruit
So wonderful as want. Feed the grape and the bean
To the vintner and the monger; I will lie down lean
With my thirst and my hunger. (*Collected Poems of Edna St. Vincent Millay*, 158)

An ancient Christian writer, Thomas à Kempis, once wrote, "Restrain from gluttony and thou shalt the more easily restrain all the inclinations of the flesh." How true it is. If we can say "no" to food, we can say "no" to a lot. He also wrote, "Whosoever knows best how to suffer will keep the greatest peace. That man is conqueror of himself, and lord of the world, the friend of Christ and heir to heaven." When we bring on ourselves the suffering of the fast, we conquer ourselves and increase our ability to allow Christ to conquer us.

Some people should not fast. If someone has low blood sugar or other physical problems, it may not be advisable for them to fast. A doctor could tell you for sure. However, for those who are able to fast, spiritual discernment, greater self-control, and obedience are the fruit of the spiritual feast of fasting (Isaiah 58:1–14).

Conclusion

We do not live in a disciplined age. It sounds quaint and remote to be talking about discipline. It seems out of step with a modern society which teaches us to deny ourselves nothing. Indulgence, however, is bondage while discipline is freedom, just as laziness is bondage and physical fitness is freedom. If Christians want to know the depth and satisfaction of spiritual experience God intends for them, they must be people of discipline.

Such discipline begins in the inner life, with meditating on the Scripture so that the Scripture can lead us, with subjecting ourselves to prayer so that Jesus can direct us, and with mastering our physical appetites so that spiritual appetites can govern us.

Speed Bump!

Slow down to be sure you've gotten the main points from this chapter.

Question   **Q1.**   What is the role of meditation in spiritual growth?

Answer   **A1.**   Meditation allows the Holy Spirit to renew the mind
and provide deep *illumination* of spiritual truth.

Q2.   What is the role of prayer in spiritual growth?

A2.   Prayer is *conversation* with God which allows for requests to be made,
communion to be experienced, and reconciliation to the will of God to
be realized.

Q3.   What is the role of fasting in spiritual growth?

A3.   Fasting allows a high level of concentration and physical deprivation
which heightens *spiritual* sensitivity.

Fill in the Blank

Question   **Q1.**   What is the role of meditation in spiritual growth?

Answer   **A1.**   Meditation allows the Holy Spirit to renew the mind
and provide deep _____ of spiritual truth.

Q2.   What is the role of prayer in spiritual growth?

A2.   Prayer is _____ with God which allows for requests to be made,
communion to be experienced, and reconciliation to the will of God to
be realized.

Q3.   What is the role of fasting in spiritual growth?

A3.   Fasting allows a high level of concentration and physical deprivation
which heightens _____ sensitivity.

For Further Thought and Discussion

---

1.   What is the hardest part about meditating for you? Finding the
passages? Memorizing the passages? Meditating on the passages? All of
the above? Have you ever given meditation an honest chance to impact
your spiritual life? What first step do you think could be taken to get
you on the road to meditation?

2.   What is the greatest hindrance to prayer for you? Is it your intellectual

struggle with prayer, or finding the time for it? What steps do you think you could take to intensify your prayer life? What help might there be from your church or other Christians?

3. Fasting is one of the last things many Christians will attempt, because it can be so uncomfortable to go without food. Have you tried fasting? Did you notice any spiritual benefit from it? The benefits are not always something you see right away. Sometimes the benefits are experienced later. Sometimes the benefits are not perceived on a sensory level. Even if it is only missing one meal, do you think you might consider fasting?

What If I Don't Believe?

If I don't believe in the benefits of the inward disciplines, I cut myself off from the very source of enlightenment and strength that form the foundation of a strong and meaningful Christian experience. I condemn myself to a mediocre walk with God.

For Further Study

1. Scripture

- Joshua 1:8
- Psalm 1:1–3
- Matthew 4:12
- Matthew 6:5–9
- Matthew 6:16–17
- Matthew 7:7–8
- Luke 18:1–8
- Acts 13:3
- Romans 12:1–2
- Colossians 4:2
- 1 Thessalonians 5:17

2. Books

The Spirit of the Disciplines, Dallas Willard
Celebration of Discipline, Richard Foster
Spiritual Disciplines for the Christian Life, Donald Whitney

No pain, no palm; no thorns, no throne; no gall, no glory; no cross, no crown.
■ **William Penn (1644–1718)**

How Do Outward Spiritual Disciplines Help Me Grow Spiritually?

Henry David Thoreau, the Boston Transcendentalist of the late 1700's, got many things wrong. He rejected Christianity and lived a very self-centered life. But in doing so, he got some things right. As one of my seminary professors used to say, even a clock that doesn't work is right twice a day.

Thoreau understood better than most of us that our inner lives shrivel from inattention, and that our outer life cannot be what it should be without sufficient attention to the inner life. Conversation degenerates into news, weather, and sports. We can only talk about what we have heard from others. We never get below the surface. Thoreau wrote that as our inner lives wither, "we go more constantly and desperately to the post office," but "the poor fellow who walks away with the greatest number of letters, proud of his extensive correspondence, has not heard from himself this long while." He concludes, "Read not *The Times*, read the Eternities."

Today, we depend not so much on the post office, but on television, cellular phones, and stereos to deaden the pain of a barren inner life. Without a rich inner life, we must fill our existence with things from "outside," and that makes for a shallow life. As we nurture our inner life, we find the television, the telephone, and the stereo to be intrusive clutter in the pursuit of the abundant life Jesus spoke of.

By disciplining our inner life and simplifying our outer life, we raise our existence to the level of joy.

What Is the Role of Simplicity in Spiritual Growth?

Simplicity is an inward reality that manifests itself in a simplified outward lifestyle that frees one from many worldly bondages.

In our increasingly complex age, simplicity is becoming a more and more admired virtue. The Amish people of mid-America have received (albeit, at times unwanted) a whole new focus of attention from American society at large in recent years, casting their simple lifestyles in a very positive light. The more conservative ones do not drive cars, have no electricity, so do not listen to the radio or watch television. They farm with horses, travel by horse and buggy, and remain, for the most part, debt free. And while no group of people is free from all problems, they are not ravaged by divorce, drugs, crime, or illegitimacy the way our society at large is. They practice a simplicity of life that has many admirable features.

Many years ago, a small religious sect known as the Shakers raised simplicity to an art form. They lived in agricultural communes and honed their simple and efficient lifestyle to the point that Shaker furniture, accessories, and artifacts are considered works of art and sell for very high prices. They sang a hymn that is enjoying a resurgence of popularity today, called the "Shaker Hymn":

'Tis the gift to be simple,
    'Tis the gift to be free,
'Tis the gift to come down where you ought to be,
    And when we find ourselves in the place just right,
'Twill be in the valley of love and delight.

When true simplicity is gained,
    To bow and to bend we shan't be ashamed.
To turn, turn will be our delight
    'Till by turning, turning, we come round right.

Simplicity is both a virtue and a blessing. A centering force in our lives, it orients us toward a right perspective on things and activities in life. It puts Jesus at the center of life, and everything else in proper perspective and proportion around Him.

This is in stark contrast to the way many of us live. Many of us are too busy, too tired, and own too much stuff. I once read a little ditty that went like this:

Possessions weigh me down in life;
I never feel quite free.
I wonder if I own my things,
Or if my things own me.

Similar poems could be written about other consuming things in our lives such as activities, burdens, and values. Do we own them, or do they own us?

We are living in a culture obsessed, possessed with a desire for outward things. In the absence of sufficient inward reality, we fill all our time and all our silence with gadgets, activities, and noise.

In this chapter we learn that . . .

1. Simplicity is an inward reality that manifests itself in a simplified outward lifestyle that frees one from many worldly bondages.
2. Solitude allows the Christian to free himself from the distraction of the world long enough to make wise, God-centered decisions and develop wise, God-centered perspectives.
3. Submission generates a trust in the sovereignty of God that frees the Christian from fear and resentment over the way others treat us, and helps build a love for others.

From a biblical perspective, our culture is sick, and conformity to a sick society is to be sick ourselves. Until we see and admit how sick, how unbalanced, how unbiblical our culture has become, we will not be able to deal with the contamination that we ourselves have absorbed.

We lack what Richard Foster, in his book *The Celebration of Discipline*, calls a divine Center—that is, a focus on God, on eternal and divine values. According to Foster, simplicity is the only thing that adequately reorients our lives so that possessions can be genuinely enjoyed without ensnaring us. Unless we have adopted the discipline of simplicity, we either fall prey to materialism (in which we must have "things" to be happy) or we fall prey to legalism (in which we consider "things" bad). Both are wrong.

The key to simplicity is to not be anxious about your life, but to "seek first the kingdom of God and His righteousness, and all these things [your life needs] shall be added to you" (Matthew 6:33). When we seek the kingdom *first*, then everything necessary will follow in its proper place. Everything depends on keeping the "first" thing "first." Even simplicity itself becomes wrong when living a simple lifestyle comes before seeking first the kingdom of God.

The philosopher/theologian Kierkegaard asked penetrating questions to sort out what was "kingdom seeking" and what was not. Should we try to exert a good influence for the kingdom through our job, or should we give away our money to the poor, or should we go out and preach the truth that people should seek the kingdom first? His answer is "no!" We should first seek the kingdom of God! All those things are secondary to seeking the kingdom.

> Then in a certain sense it is nothing I shall do. Yes, certainly, in a certain sense it is nothing, become nothing before God, learn to keep silent; in this silence is the beginning, which is, *first* to seek God's Kingdom (87).

Foster goes on to explain that freedom from anxiety is one of the inward evidences that we are seeking first the kingdom of God. When we are, we have a settled lack of concern for possessions. Neither the greedy nor the miserly know this liberty; it has nothing to do with wealth or poverty. It is an inward spirit of trust. A person living without things is not necessarily living in simplicity. Nor is the presence of wealth a sign that a person has abandoned simplicity. The whole question revolves around what we are trusting for our security and meaning, and what we do with what we have.

Freedom from anxiety results from seeking first the kingdom of God.

Freedom from anxiety is characterized by three inner attitudes. To receive what we have as a gift from God is the first inner attitude of simplicity. Second, we are to know that it is God's business, and not ours, to care for what we have. Third, we are to have our goods available to others. When we do these three things we are in a position not "to be anxious" and we have taken the first crucial steps toward the Christian discipline of simplicity.

By this we see that a life of simplicity has not only to do with our possessions, but also with our time and activities. Certainly, we have possessions that it would be hard to live without. I couldn't easily write this book, for example, without my computer and other books. But the question is whether the things we own are tools to be used in the pursuit of kingdom life, or whether we just accumulate "things" to try to bring happiness to our lives.

Why I Need to Know This

Simplicity is not a natural or cultural virtue. By learning that it is a biblical virtue, I am more likely to acquire it. Solitude is similar. It is almost never seen as a practical virtue, yet the benefits of it are obvious. By learning more about it, I may be able to gain the simplicity and solitude in my life necessary to lead an unfrazzled life. Finally, both by nature and by enculturation, we tend not to submit to others. Yet by not doing so, we can remain in bondage to our emotions when others hurt us.

The same question could be asked about activities. Are the things that keep us busy important to God? Do we move purposefully through life, focusing on kingdom priorities, rejecting incidentals, or are we caught up in the tyranny of the urgent, running doggedly from one activity to the next in the pursuit of things that are not kingdom priorities?

We are to have those possessions and engage in those activities that reflect our kingdom priorities. We ought to be able to look through our home, our garage, our basement, our attic, our calendar, and our checkbook register, and justify everything in each of these places in light of the kingdom of Christ.

Nothing we have or do must violate the values of the kingdom of God. Are there books, magazines, television programs that do not reflect kingdom values? They need to go. Are there activities on the schedule that do not reflect the kingdom of God? They need to go. Everything we have, everything we do must reflect the values of the kingdom of God.

Even when we have gotten rid of things that ought not to be there, we are still sometimes left with the task of choosing between two good things. That is, we may not be doing anything that dishonors God, but we are still too busy. In that case, we must eliminate something, even if it is a good thing. God does not want us to live frazzled lives nor does He want our possessions to own us. So we are all forced to omit good things from our lives in the name of sane living. It is hard to do. That is why it is a spiritual *discipline*

What Is the Role of Solitude in Spiritual Growth?

Solitude allows the Christian to free himself from the distraction of the world long enough to make wise, God-centered decisions and develop wise, God-centered perspectives.

In Mark 1:35, Jesus had just spent an exhausting time casting out demons and healing sick people. "Now in the morning, having risen a long while before daylight, [Jesus] went out and departed to a solitary place; and there He prayed."

Later in Mark 6:31, 32, after John the Baptist was murdered (an emotionally trying event), and after the apostles gathered to Jesus to tell Him all the things they had done and taught on their missionary assignments, Jesus said, "Come aside by yourselves to a deserted place and rest a while." So many people had been making demands on their time that they didn't even have time to eat, so they went to a deserted place and rested.

Jesus and His disciples made solitary time a priority.

Blaise Pascal wrote in his work, *Pensées*:

I have often said that the sole cause of man's unhappiness is that he does not know how to stay quietly in his room. . . . What people want is not the easy peaceful life that allows us to think of our unhappy condition, nor the dangers of war, nor the burdens of office, but the agitation that takes our mind off it and diverts us. That is why we prefer the hunt to the capture. That is why men are so fond of hustle and bustle; that is why prison is such a fearful punishment; that is why the pleasures of solitude are so incomprehensible.

We are not used to solitude. If we have no sufficient inner life to sustain us, we must fill the void, the time, the silence, with activity, music, TV, noise. We cannot bear to be alone. But there is joy in solitude if we can but wean ourselves from the input of the world and attune ourselves to the input that comes from God.

If we are going to live lives of purpose, meaning, and satisfaction, we must learn to be quiet. We must learn to be alone. We must learn to draw inner strength, personal strength, divine strength, from being alone and being quiet. Thinking. **We must learn to be alone and to be quiet.** Listening to see if God is going to plant a seed in our heart or mind that we would miss if we didn't stop to be quiet. Theologian and philosopher Kierkegaard once said, "If I were a doctor and were asked for my advice, I should reply, 'Create silence.' "

Is there something knocking on the door of your mind or heart, calling you to something you have not yet perceived, hinting that there is more to life than you have experienced? I believe it is God. So get alone. Get quiet. Listen. Thoughts, ideas, values, desires will come to you that, like timid rabbits, do not come out when surrounded by hustle and bustle, but which will hop out into the open and sit there to be noticed when all gets quiet.

In his book, *Half Time*, Bob Buford writes of evaluating your life at mid-life and making necessary and desirable changes. The biggest mistake most of us make in the first half of our lives is not taking enough time on the really important things. He writes:

> A while ago I had the pleasure of meeting Konosuke Matsushita, chairman of the huge and highly successful Japanese electronics company bearing his last name. Matsushita follows the practice, not uncommon in Asia, of retreating to his garden from time to time in order to live a contemplative and reflective life. When Matsushita walks into a room, the awe is palpable. Without saying a word, he bespeaks a powerful centeredness and elegant reserve (67).

Oh, that it might be said of all Christians because they have spent quiet time with God.

Solitude is not merely being alone. It is also a frame of mind you assume when you are alone. And it is not something you do once, once a week, or once a month. It is a mind-set of spending sufficient solitude to orient your life to God, however much time it takes.

During your quiet times with God, it is helpful, after prayer and Scripture reading, to do something to engage the mind. You can ask the Lord to plant in your mind anything He would like to be there. You might ask yourself some important questions, such as:

- If Jesus were sitting before me in this very room, what would He most like to say to me?

- What does God want from me that He does not yet have?

- What am I living for? Is it worth it?

- What do I want out of life, believing it to be God's will?

- Am I willing to pay the price for it, realizing God does not give us things without self-involvement?

- Who am I? Do I realize how much I am loved and accepted by God? What would Jesus say to me about His unconditional love for me if He were to appear to me now?

- What do I want my tombstone to say about me?

- What motivates me?

- If I could do anything in the world, what would I like to do for God?

- What gifts has He given me that I should be using?

- What am I willing to die for?

- How important are people to me? How do I show that importance? How can I make people a greater part of my life?

- What can I change to make my life better?

- What can I do to free myself to serve God more completely?

- What can I do to be a better person?

- How can I be more like the person I most admire?

- What steps do I need to take to make the rest of my life better than what I have already lived?

You might consider keeping a journal in which to record your inner journey. Make it what Buford calls "the relentless search for the most noble, decent part of me." Listen to God. He will speak through Scripture, through thoughts, through desires, through other people. Write down your good thoughts. Follow through on your good ideas. One of my former pastors used to say, "Follow your good impulses. It is probably the Holy Spirit."

What Is the Role of Submission in Spiritual Growth?

Submission generates a trust in the sovereignty of God that frees the Christian from fear and resentment over the way others treat us, and helps build a love for others.

Martin Luther, father of the Reformation in 1517, succinctly stated the balance that the Christian must keep regarding submission: "A Christian is a perfectly free lord of all, subject to none. A Christian is a perfectly dutiful servant of all, subject to everyone." The Christian is free, but is to use his freedom to serve others.

Since every discipline has a corresponding freedom, we can identify the freedom in submission as being released from the terrible burden of always needing to get our own way. The other evening, my wife and I were in a restaurant when a father, mother, and five-year-old child came in. The parents wanted to sit one place in the restaurant and the child wanted to sit someplace else. The parents won, but paid a terrible price for the victory. The child wailed and lamented and fussed and complained until the entire restaurant had a headache. But most miserable was the child. He was a slave to his desires and will. If he could not get his way, his life collapsed, and all was lost.

He is in for a disgruntled life, because few of us get our way nearly as often as we need to to be happy if our happiness depends on getting our own way. As adults, we often fuss and stew, make bad decisions, and run roughshod over other people when we don't get our way. Or we may withdraw, become resentful and bitter, and develop an ulcer—all because we demand our own way and are not free to give up. With the discipline of submission, we can be free to drop it all and gain the wonderful freedom of not always having to get our own way.

Almost all family quarrels, almost all work-related conflict, almost all church fights and splits occur because people do not have the freedom to give up their rights—perceived or real—to others. Often we do not yield to others because, in the heat of the battle, we are convinced that an important principle is at stake.

Most things in life are *not* major issues.

And perhaps there is. But other important principles are also at stake: the principle of unity among Christians; the principle of mutual submission; and the principle of considering others as more important than yourself. Often, if a wise third party is consulted, or when the issue blows over and time gives us more perspective, we realize that while a principle was at stake, other more important principles were also at stake, and we violated the more important ones in favor of the less important one simply because we wanted to win.

Only when we have learned the discipline of submission can we come to the place where a selfish spirit no longer controls us. Only submission can free us to distinguish between genuine issues and stubborn self-will. Most things in life are not major issues. If we could see this and accept it, we could hold those things lightly. Often the best way to handle these issues is to say nothing and let enough time pass that perspective is gained.

William Booth, founder of the Salvation Army, was once brought to an international meeting when he was very old and infirm. Though too weak to give an address, a microphone was brought to him, and he said one word several times as his final message to the huge, international organization that the Salvation Army had by then become. What was that word? We would expect it to be a terribly important word, given the situation. The word? "Others. Others. Others."

We find submission easiest when we begin to truly value other people. When we truly place an importance on other people created in the image of God and those for whom Christ died, when we truly comprehend that God wants to use us to touch the lives of others, then we find submission easier and easier to manifest.

Ephesians 5:22—6:9 gives us three sets of relationships in which people are in submission to one another. The husband is in submission to the needs of the wife, while the wife is in submission to the authority of her husband (5:22–33). The parents are in submission to the needs of the children while the children are in submission to the authority of the parents (6:1–4). Masters are in submission to the needs of the slave while the slave is in submission to the authority of the master (5–9). This is the pattern God wants to see: all in submission to the needs of those under them, and all in submission to the authority of those over them. This brings about true divine unity and harmony.

We must be in submission both to those under us and to those over us.

Of course, a word of balance is needed here. We do no one any favors if we allow them to run roughshod over us or others. If we are in a position of leadership we often cannot allow a foolish or destructive plan to be implemented in the name of peace when it would bring harm in the long run to others. But even then, if we have a spirit of submission, we are able to assert our decision or proper course of action with a spirit of love, respect, and deference.

When does submission go too far? When it is destructive. Peter calls on Christians to be submissive to those in authority over us (1 Peter 2:13, 14), yet when the government of his day commanded him to stop preaching Christ, Peter answered, "Whether it is right in the sight of God to listen to you more than to God, you judge. For we cannot but speak the things which we have seen and heard" (Acts 4:19–20).

In another epistle, Paul called us to obey the governing authorities over us (Romans 13:1), yet when he saw that the state was failing to fulfill its God-ordained function of providing justice for all, he held it accountable and insisted that the wrong be corrected (Acts 16:37).

When submission results in a violation of other biblical commands or principles, we must resist, though with a Christ-like spirit.

With that word of caution and balance, however, we can finish with the areas in which we should practice submission: first, we submit to the Triune God; second, to the Scripture; third, to our family; fourth, to our neighbors; fifth, to the believing community; sixth to the disadvantaged; and finally, to the world. In each of these contexts we submit ourselves to others and seek to be used as an instrument of God to bring the gospel, healing, and peace.

Conclusion

The outward disciplines—those disciplines that govern our relationship with people, possessions, and circumstances around us—grow out of the inner disciplines. Without the inner disciplines, we cannot hope to sustain the outward ones. Built upon the foundation of the inner disciplines, however, the outer disciplines free us from the tyranny and bondage to things, to needing always to be right, and to always having to get our own way.

Speed Bump!

Slow down to be sure you've gotten the main points of this chapter.

Question   **Q1.**   What is the role of simplicity in spiritual growth?

Answer   **A1.**   Simplicity is an inward reality that manifests itself in a simplified outward *lifestyle* that frees one from many worldly bondages.

Q2. What is the role of solitude in spiritual growth?

A2. Solitude allows the Christian to free himself from the *distraction* of the world long enough to make wise, God-centered decisions and develop wise, God-centered perspectives.

Q3. What is the role of submission in spiritual growth?

A3. Submission generates a trust in the *sovereignty* of God that frees the Christian from fear and resentment over the way others treat us, and helps build a love for others.

Fill in the Blank

Q1. What is the role of simplicity in spiritual growth?

A1. Simplicity is an inward reality that manifests itself in a simplified outward _____ that frees one from many worldly bondages.

Q2. What is the role of solitude in spiritual growth?

A2. Solitude allows the Christian to free himself from the _____ of the world long enough to make wise, God-centered decisions and develop wise, God-centered perspectives.

Q3. What is the role of submission in spiritual growth?

A3. Submission generates a trust in the _____ of God that frees the Christian from fear and resentment over the way others treat us, and helps build a love for others.

For Further Thought and Discussion

1. Do you think simplicity means that you cannot make a lot of money and that you must live oddly, by the world's standards? If not, how would you describe simplicity in your own words?

2. Have you ever spent time alone in a place of beautiful scenery and come away refreshed and strengthened? What do you think is the secret to have the same result without necessarily going to some beautiful, faraway place?

3. What do you think is the greatest stumbling block in most people's minds regarding the discipline of submission? What do you think could be done to overcome that stumbling block?

What If I Don't Believe?

If I don't believe, I will miss out on some of the lifestyle changes most necessary to live an unfrazzled life. Until I can be freed from the tyrannies of money, a too-busy schedule, and other people's treatment, I will be at the mercy of circumstances for my fulfillment in life.

For Further Study

1. Scripture

- Matthew 6:19–34
- Mark 6:31–32
- Ephesians 5:21—6:9

2. Books

The Spirit of the Disciplines, Dallas Willard
Celebration of Discipline, Richard Foster
Spiritual Disciplines for the Christian Life, Donald Whitney

I never made a sacrifice. We ought not to talk of sacrifice when we remember the great sacrifice that he made who left His Father's throne on high to give himself for us.
■ David Livingstone (1813–1873)

How Do Corporate Spiritual Disciplines Help Me Grow Spiritually?

Some things we need to do alone and some things we need to do with other people. We paint alone; we play tennis with other people. We brush our teeth alone; we go to the symphony with other people. We vote alone; we go to ball games with other people.

In the same way, we do some of the spiritual disciplines alone, and we do some with other people. That leads us to our third type of spiritual discipline, the corporate disciplines. The first two types of spiritual discipline involve things we do alone. While there is a solitary dimension about the corporate disciplines, we also do them with other people.

What Is the Role of Confession in Spiritual Growth?

Repentance and confession restore moral integrity and authority.

Confession is the admission that one has done, said, or thought something wrong. Some of us toy with confession. We are like the man who sent a check to the IRS. He said he owed them money and couldn't sleep, so he was sending them a check for $500. If he still couldn't sleep, he said he'd send the rest!

It is difficult for some people to acknowledge to themselves that they are wrong and must face the consequences. It is even harder to confess to God they are wrong. It is virtually impossible to admit to others they are wrong The tongue and lips are al most unable to form the words, "I'm sorry. I was wrong. Please forgive me."

Yet confession isn't a halfway station. We must go all the way. Without confession we lose our fellowship with God, we forfeit our personal integrity (because of a guilty conscience), and we sacrifice our moral authority (because of a hypocritical reputation). In serious spiritual battles, it may be advantageous or even necessary to confess sins to another or publicly.

Private Confession

The first step in confession is private confession. We must acknowledge to ourselves that we have sinned, and we must confess that sin to God. The apostle John wrote, "If we say that we have no sin, we deceive ourselves, and the truth is not in us. If we confess our sins, He is faithful and just to forgive us our sins and to cleanse us from all unrighteousness" (1 John 1:8–9). David wrote,

> Blessed is he whose transgression is forgiven, / Whose sin is covered. / Blessed is the man to whom the Lord does not impute iniquity, / And in whose spirit there is no deceit. / When I kept silent, my bones grew old / Through my groaning all the day long. / For day and night Your hand was heavy upon me; / My vitality was turned into the drought of summer. / Selah. I acknowledged my sin to You, / And my iniquity I have not hidden. / I said, "I will confess my transgressions to the Lord," / And You forgave the iniquity of my sin (Psalm 32:1–5).

Unconfessed sin does not jeopardize our salvation. But it does interrupt our fellowship, our relationship with God. And it does undermine our moral authority. When we know that we have done something wrong and do not make it right with Him, we are merely playing games with God. We also have to hide it from others.

Confession ought to occur as soon as we realize we have sinned. It may be that we did something we did not know was sin, and we learned later from the Bible or heard from someone that it was sin. Or perhaps we knew it was sin and did it anyway. When the Holy Spirit convicts us of our sin, that is when we admit it and confess it to God, agreeing with Him that it was sin.

In this chapter we learn that . . .

1. Repentance and confession restore moral integrity and authority.
2. Worship is a responsibility of the Christian which, if taken seriously, will be deepened in his relationship with God.
3. Generosity requires and encourages a detachment from the things of this world, and demonstrates living for the next world.

I have found it very helpful to pray Scripture back to the Lord when confessing sin. The primary passages are, of course, 1 John 1:8–9 and Psalm 32:1–5. They also include Psalm 51:1–13 and Psalm 103:8–14. Read these passages back to the Lord as though you were the one speaking them for the very first time, making adjustments in the exact wording so that the Scripture becomes first-person prayer.

This practice not only gives you an idea of what to say, but also helps you see that great men in the Bible sinned and had to confess it (perhaps greater sin than you have ever committed), and that the Lord is most willing to forgive you.

Being convicted of sin might be emotionally painful, and when you confess it, the pain might not go away instantly. That does not necessarily mean that anything was wrong with your confession; our emotions often do not come down to earth as quickly as our intellect does. It might take time to begin to feel forgiven.

Personal confession of sin is essential to keep a clear conscience and to have moral authority. If we do not have a clear conscience, our guilty conscience condemns us whenever we try to think or act spiritually.

Also, if we do not confess sin our heart hardens to it, and it is easier to sin next time, and harder to confess next time. As a result we **Our heart hardens to unconfessed sin.** drift from God and a desire for spiritual things. A callus gets worn on the soul, preventing it from functioning as it ought. It does not commune with God as it ought. It no longer enjoys spiritual things as it should. Just as calluses on the hands of a brain surgeon would impede the very basic functioning of life for him, so calluses on the soul from unconfessed sin disrupt the very basic functioning of life for the Christian.

Public Confession

Often, our confession must go further than only admitting to ourselves and to God that we have sinned. Sometimes we must confess our sins to others because we need to or because we want to.

Why I Need to Know This

Repentance and confession are essential to a healthy Christian experience. If I don't keep my life free of sin, I am condemned to root around in the mire of guilt, hampered in my relationship with God and others. I need to know that worship is a twenty-four-hour a day thing, and that if I am not getting what I want out of my worship times, I probably need to look at the rest of my time. Finally, I must cross the last barrier of commitment to the Lord—namely, giving generously to the work of the ministry.

First of all, let us look at the times we need to confess our sins to others. If we wrong someone else in word or deed, we need to confess it to the person. There are eight words that will correct the sin, if spoken sincerely: "I'm sorry. I was wrong. Please forgive me." Nothing else will correct it. Time may cover it over, or dull or stop the pain. But only forgiveness will make it go away. The other person may forgive you without your asking. That is wonderful. Yet, in order for you to know that the slate is clean between you, you need to confess the sin.

One good rule of thumb that makes sense to me is to confess the sin to whoever was involved. That is, if you sin against one person privately, you need only to confess it to that one person. For example, I once cheated on an exam. Later I felt terrible about it. I went back to the teacher and confessed the sin to him and volunteered to take whatever consequences he felt were just. That is as far as the matter needed to go.

If the sin is against many people and very public, then the confession may need to be a public one. I know of a young lady who got pregnant out of wedlock. Embarrassed, she quit coming to church for a while, but then, out of terrible loneliness and iso-lation, she wanted to return. She confessed her sin to the Lord, and then to the pastor and elders of the church, asking if she could be restored to fellowship. Of course her request was granted. However, the members of the church did not know how to respond to her.

So one Sunday, with full agreement of the young lady, the pastor announced to the congregation that this young lady was pregnant out of wedlock but she had repented of her sin to God and had confessed her sin to the pastor and elders. Now, to make the process complete, she was confessing her sin to the entire church and asking them to forgive her and restore her to their fellowship.

A very healing time in the church followed because it allowed the girl to feel forgiven and the members of the church to open their hearts to her in full love and compassion.

Confession, when done properly, brings about healing, freedom, and restoration as nothing else can.

Sometimes we *need* to confess our sins, and other times we may *want* to confess our sins on a level beyond what is ordinarily considered necessary. For example, there may be times after we have sinned badly that we need help believing God will forgive us. In such times, it may be beneficial to seek out a mature and trusted Christian whom you can tell about the sin, and have the person talk through the Scriptures with you and reassure you of what you already may know—that God loves you and forgives you. I know from experience and from the testimony of others that it is often helpful to have that truth verified by a trusted spiritual mentor.

We also may want to confess our sin beyond normal bounds when we are having trouble breaking free of a given sin. In such times, it may be useful to seek out a mature and trusted spiritual mentor to support you and hold you accountable. A man once came up to me and told me he had struck his wife the week before. He didn't want to ever do that again, and asked me to question him periodically how things were going with his wife. It was a wise move. Usually, when we think that no one will ever know about our sin, we feel freer to persist in it. When someone else knows, often that alone is enough to break the hold the sin has over us.

Confession done properly heals, frees, and restores.

I want to close by describing two different experiences I have had with confession. One was during an Institute in Basic Life Principles seminar by Bill Gothard. He taught about the importance of a cleansed conscience, and encouraged us to have a time alone when we asked the Lord to bring to our conscious minds anyone we had wronged and not made it right, or anyone who had wronged us and we had not forgive them. He suggested we make a list.

I did. I forgave everyone who had wronged me, though I still have to reiterate and renew that forgiveness occasionally. Then, I went down through the (lamentably long) list, contacted everyone on the list that I could, asked them to forgive me, and offered to make restitution when appropriate. I felt cleansed, free, and stronger. It was a practice I have maintained ever since, and I consider it one of the crucial spiritual exercises of my Christian life.

In a similar process, I have made it a practice to go through the seven steps to freedom suggested in the writings of Neil Anderson. In this process, we ask the Lord to impress on our mind anything we have ever done that might give the spiritual forces of darkness an advantage in our lives. Then, one by one, in prayer, we repudiate them and ask for the Lord's strength in the spiritual war Each time, I feel cleansed, free, and stronger.

Confession of sin is a lost art in many churches. Yet it is such a powerful practice that it must be considered one of the key spiritual disciplines.

What Is the Role of Worship in Spiritual Growth?

Worship is a responsibility of the Christian which, if taken seriously, will be deepened in his relationship with God.

Worship is not always easy. Sometimes it is hard work, both on an individual and corporate level. On the personal level, it is hard to get up regularly every morning for a time of personal worship. Even if you do, it is hard to know what to do, and to have it be consistently meaningful.

On a corporate level, worship can be equally difficult. The church service you attend may not readily encourage your worship. Worse yet, it may discourage it. Nevertheless, we are admonished in Scripture to worship God.

In worship, we

engage ourselves with, dwell upon, and express the greatness, beauty, and goodness of God through thought and the use of words, rituals and symbols. We do this alone as well as in union with God's people. To worship is to see God as worthy, to ascribe great worth to Him (Willard, 177).

We see pure worship in Revelation 4:11, "You are worthy, O Lord, to receive glory and honor and power; for You created all things, and by Your will they exist and were created."

Again, we see in 5:12, 13, "Worthy is the Lamb who was slain to receive power and riches and wisdom, and strength and honor and glory and blessing! Blessing and honor and glory and power be to Him who sits on the throne, and to the Lamb, forever and ever!"

As we worship in this manner, giving careful attention to the details of God's actions and to his "worthiness," the good we adore enters our minds and hearts to increase our faith and strengthen us to be as he is (Willard, 178).

My first question, when it comes to facing my responsibility, profound privilege, and opportunity to worship, is "What do I do?"

That isn't the right question.

Worship is not so much what we do, but the mind and heart and spirit with which we do it. Certainly there are things we should do. We can carve out the time to spend alone with God personally, on a regular (daily is best) basis. We can be sure we get our bodies out of bed on Sunday morning and go to church. In that sense, worship is a discipline. We *do* have actions we must do.

However, whether or not worship actually happens depends on what we do with the nearly sixteen to eighteen hours we have in a day. If our thoughts are not centered meaningfully on God the rest of the time, our worship will not be centered meaningfully on God. One reason worship is a spiritual discipline is because it involves a disciplined way of living that goes beyond the times we may set aside for formal worship.

The most important avenue to meaningful worship is the focus of the inner life on God. We are to live centered inward on the indwelling God, so that He is the source of our **True worship springs from a disciplined way of living.** words, thoughts, and actions. If we are accustomed to carrying out the business of our lives in human strength and wisdom, we will usually do the same in worship.

François Fénelon writes, "Happy the soul which by a sincere self-renunciation, holds itself ceaselessly in the hands of its Creator, ready to do everything which he wishes; which never stops saying to itself a hundred times a day, 'Lord, what wouldst thou that I should do?' "

Driving to work, we ask our Teacher, "How are we doing?" Immediately, our Mentor flashes before our mind that caustic remark we made to our spouse at breakfast, that shrug of disinterest we gave our children on the way out the door. We realize we have been living in the flesh. There is confession, restoration, and a new humility.

We stop at the gas station and sense a divine urging to get acquainted with the attendant, to see her as a person rather than an automaton. We drive on, rejoicing in our new insight into Spirit-initiated activity. As so it goes throughout our day: a prompting here or a drawing there, sometimes a bolting ahead or a lagging behind our Guide. Like a child taking first steps we are learning through success and failure, confident that we have a present Teacher who, through the Holy Spirit, will guide us into all truth. In this way we come to understand what Paul means when he instructs us to "walk not according to the flesh but according to the Spirit" (Romans 8:4). (Foster, 167).

When we live each hour of the day in fellowship and communion with the Lord and take that attitude into our worship experiences, we find richer, more meaningful worship.

What Is the Role of Generosity in Spiritual Growth?

Generosity requires and encourages a detachment from the things of this world, and demonstrates living for the next world.

The manner in which a Christian handles his money indicates the level of his spiritual maturity. God, of course, does not need our money. He has no need of gold, but if He did, He could speak tons of it into existence. So why does He ask us to give our money away for His causes? Well, He wants our hearts, and one of the primary ways He uses to see if He has our hearts is to see how we use our money. If He has our hearts, He will also have our money. If He doesn't have our money, He does not yet have our hearts.

Most people are not willing to give money away until they have achieved a certain level of detachment from this world. If we are living for this world, what would possess us to give away our money? It is the root of power in this world, the primary source of getting what this world has to offer. But if we have matured to the point that we are willing, even desirous, of living for the next world, then giving our money away is not such an incredible thing. As Jesus said, our hearts will be where our treasures are (Luke 12:34).

There are at least six major reasons why we ought to exercise the spiritual discipline of generosity.

Obedience: The Bible makes it clear in a host of passages that God expects us to be generous with our money, to give to others in need, and to contribute to the spread of the gospel and the furtherance of the kingdom of God. We can either obey or disobey this expectation. (See 2 Corinthians 9:7.)

Citizenship: We are citizens of another world and another kingdom. We are to lay up treasures in heaven, our real home. (See Matthew 6:19–21.)

Worship: Giving is an act of worship. We give of our money to demonstrate our devotion to God. Each time we go to a worship service, we ought to give some money. Certainly, we can give one check a month to cover our tithes and offerings, but that means we would go to church a number of times without giving anything. In my opinion, it is better to give a fourth of our gift each week than to give it all once a month or once a year. And we ought to give it as an act of worship. (See Philippians 4:18.)

Trust: Giving money reflects our trust in God's provision. It reflects our belief that God takes care of us. We do not take care of ourselves. Our employer does not take care of us. Especially when we do not have what we need, we show trust in God when we give our money to His causes. (See Mark 12:41–44.)

Trustworthiness: Our giving demonstrates to God that we can be trusted. Scripture teaches that if someone can be trusted in little things, he is then worthy of being entrusted with greater things. (See Luke 16:10–13.)

Blessing: When we give, we become eligible for God's blessing in our lives on a level greater than if we don't give. I am not suggesting that God gives us financial reward for financial giving. The prosperity gospel is a false teaching. God does not promise financial prosperity for financial generosity. He promises spiritual prosperity for financial generosity. (See 2 Corinthians 9:6–8.)

Even when we agree with these arguments, it is still sometimes hard to give money away. Often it is hardest for the very poor and very rich. The very poor often do not want to give any money away because every penny they give away takes away from their life necessities. The very rich often do not want to give money away because they want even more money. Studies have shown that the richer Americans are, the smaller percentage of their money they give away. Ten percent of twenty-five thousand dollars is only two thousand, five hundred dollars. It may be a lot of money if you don't have much, but it will not change one's standard of living. However, ten percent of five hundred thousand dollars is fifty thousand dollars. That will buy a new luxury car. Often the rich would rather have the new car.

Most of us are in the middle between the very rich and the very poor, but we still have problems with giving. In fact, we often have trouble giving for both reasons. We think that giving keeps us from necessities as well as luxuries. If so, we must exercise the discipline to give our money to things that will advance the kingdom of God.

Conclusion

Spiritual growth is a mysterious, mystical result of the cooperative work between God and Christian. The Christian cannot grow spiritually without the initiating work of God, but God will not give the spiritual growth without a response from the Christian. This apparent paradox is stated most clearly in Philippians 2:12–13, where the apostle Paul wrote, "Work out your own salvation with fear and trembling; for it is God who works in you both to will and to do for His good pleasure." Therefore, the Christian cannot passively trust in God and wait on Him to bring about spiritual maturity. The Christian must *do* things in order to grow spiritually.

The desired goal of discipline is freedom.

That, of course, is the whole point of spiritual disciplines. In addition to all the things a Christian must *know, understand,* and *believe* in the process of growing spiritually, he must also engage in the spiritual disciplines in order to grow.

The desired goal of the disciplines is freedom. They are not intended to limit us or restrict us or hamper us. They are intended to give us the strength and insight to do the things we want to do. Just as the athlete's physical regimen is not intended to limit her but to give her freedom to excel in her chosen field, so the Christian's spiritual regimen is intended to give her freedom to excel in her walk with God.

Freedom, however, doesn't come by knowing the disciplines, or understanding them, or believing them. Freedom comes by doing them.

Every discipline has its corresponding freedom. If I have schooled myself in the art of rhetoric, I am free to deliver a moving speech when the occasion requires it. Demosthenes was free to be an orator only because he had gone through the discipline of speaking above the ocean roar with pebbles in his mouth. The purpose of the disciplines is freedom. Our aim is the freedom, not the discipline. The moment we make the discipline our central focus, we turn it into law and lose the corresponding freedom.

Engaging in the disciplines realizes a greater good. In and of themselves they are of no value whatsoever. They serve only as a means of setting us before God so that He can liberate us. The liberation is the end; the disciplines are merely the means. They are not the answer; they only lead us to the Answer. We must clearly understand this limitation of the disciplines if we are to avoid bondage. Not only must we understand, but we need to consistently remind ourselves of it lest we yield to the severe temptation to center on the disciplines. Let us forever center on Christ and view the spiritual disciplines as a way of drawing us closer to His heart.

Speed Bump!

Slow down to be sure you've gotten the main points of this chapter.

Question **A**nswer

Q1. What is the role of confession in spiritual growth?

A1. Repentance and confession *restore* moral integrity and authority.

Q2. What is the role of worship in spiritual growth?

A2. Worship is a responsibility of the Christian which, if taken seriously, will be *deepened* in his relationship with God.

Q3. What is the role of generosity in spiritual growth?

A3. Generosity requires and encourages a *detachment* from the things of this world, and demonstrates living for the next world.

Fill in the Blank

Question
Answer

Q1. What is the role of confession in spiritual growth?

A1. Repentance and confession _____ moral integrity and authority.

Q2. What is the role of worship in spiritual growth?

A2. Worship is a responsibility of the Christian which, if taken seriously, will be _____ in his relationship with God.

Q3. What is the role of generosity in spiritual growth?

A3. Generosity requires and encourages a _____ from the things of this world, and demonstrates living for the next world.

For Further Thought and Discussion

1. Have you ever gone through a fearless and relentless inventory of your inner life to see what is missing that the Lord would like to be there, and what is there that the Lord would like see missing? What is the most intimidating thing about doing that? What is the most promising thing about it?

2. On a scale of one to ten, how satisfying do you find personal worship? Corporate worship? How much of the disappointment do you think might be a result of how you use the rest of your time? What could you do to enrich your worship?

3. Is it hard for you to give a percentage of your money to the Lord? If so, why? If not, how did you come to the point of freedom?

What If I Don't Believe?

If I don't believe, I cut myself off from the disciplines that help me have the best relationships with others. If I don't believe I need to keep "confessed up" with the Lord and others, I forfeit my relationship with God and my moral authority with others. If I don't order my whole life so that worship is meaningful, I lose out on worship, one of the great hungers of my life, and I sacrifice the benefits of a well-ordered life. Finally, if I never get emancipated from the tyranny of wanting money, I will never be free to experience the heights of spiritual existence as I join God and the church in reaching the world for Christ.

For Further Study

1. Scripture

- Matthew 6:19–21

- Luke 12:34

- John 4:24

- 1 John 1:9

- Revelation 4—5

2. Books

The Spirit of the Disciplines, Dallas Willard
Celebration of Discipline, Richard Foster
Spiritual Disciplines for the Christian Life, Donald Whitney
What You Need to Know About Spiritual Warfare, Max Anders (The reader
   may find helpful the chapter on cleansing the conscience.)

Bibliography

Bounds, E. M. *The Essentials of Prayer.* Chicago: Moody Press, 1980.

Brand, Paul. *Fearfully and Wonderfully Made.* Grand Rapids: Zondervan, 1987.

Buford, Robert. *Half Time.* Grand Rapids: Zondervan. 1994.

Calvin, John. *Institutes of the Christian Religion.* Grand Rapids: Eerdmans, 1949.

Carmichael, Amy. *Toward Jerusalem.* London: Society for Promoting Christian Knowledge, 1936.

Crabb, Lawrence. *Encouragement: The Key to Caring.* Grand Rapids: Zondervan, 1984.

Dickens, Charles. *A Christmas Carol.* Philadelphia: Lippincott, 1915.

Foster, Richard. *The Celebration of Discipline.* San Francisco: Harper & Row, 1978.

Franklin, Benjamin. *Benjamin Franklin: His Life.* New Haven: Yale University Press, 1964.

Gray, Alice. *Stories for the Heart.* Gresham, Ore.: Vision House, 1996.

Herriot, James. *All Things Wise and Wonderful.* New York: St. Martins Press, 1976.

Hitt, Russell. *How Christians Grow.* New York: Oxford University Press, 1979.

Hybels, Bill. *Too Busy Not to Pray.* Downers Grove, Ill.: InterVarsity Press, 1988.

Lewis, C. S. *Surprised by Joy.* New York: Harcourt, 1956.

Packer, James I. *Rediscovering Holiness.* Ann Arbor: Servant Publications, 1992.

Plantiga, Cornelius. *Not the Way It's Supposed to Be.* Grand Rapids: Eerdmans, 1995.

Schaeffer, Francis. *True Spirituality.* Wheaton, Ill.: Tyndale House, 1971.

Ten Boom, Corrie. *Tramp for the Lord.* Old Tappan, N.J.: Fleming H. Revell, 1974.

Whitney, Donald. *Spiritual Disciplines for the Christian Life.* Colorado Springs, Colo.: NavPress, 1991.

Willard, Dallas. *The Spirit of the Disciplines.* San Francisco: Harper & Row, 1988.

Master Review

Chapter 1

Q1. What is the beginning point for spiritual growth?

A1. The beginning point for spiritual growth is to be spiritually *born again*.

Q2. What is the significance of being in Christ?

A2. Being in Christ means that we are *joint-heirs* with Him and recipients of the eternal kindness which God intends to bestow on His children.

Chapter 2

Q1. What does the Bible teach about my spiritual growth?

A1. The Bible teaches that all spiritual growth *begins* with the work of God in my life.

Q2. What does God do for me in my spiritual life?

A2. In my spiritual life, God makes it *possible* for me gradually to know, become, and do everything He requires of me.

Q3. How do I balance my spiritual life?

A3. I balance my spiritual life by actively pursuing spiritual growth while resting in the fact that *God* alone gives spiritual growth.

Q4. How can I cope with failure?

A4. I cope with failure by accepting that while God wants me to grow spiritually, He knows I will often fail, and so does not demand *perfect* behavior from me.

Chapter 3

Q1. What are my responsibilities in spiritual growth?

A1. I must *pursue* mature knowledge, character, and ministry.

Q2. What is our motivation for obedience to God?

A2. Our motivation for obedience to God is our *love* for Him who first loved us.

Q3. What is my goal in spiritual growth?

A3. My goal in spiritual growth is to become progressively more like *Christ.*

Q4. What is the danger in pursuing spiritual growth?

A4. The danger in pursuing spiritual growth is trying to find spiritual satisfaction *our* way instead of God's way.

Chapter 4

Q1. What role does the Bible play in spiritual growth?

A1. The Bible *enlightens* and *empowers* me to grow spiritually.

Q2. Why do we need the Bible?

A2. We need the Bible for *meaningful* life on earth and for hope for *eternal* life.

Q3. How should we respond to the Bible?

A3. Our response to the Bible should be *total obedience* to it.

Chapter 5

Q1. Why do I need other believers?

A1. I need other believers because God has created me to live in *mutual* dependence and fellowship with them.

Q2. What is my responsibility to give to other Christians?

A2. My responsibility to other Christians is to *love* them and *serve* them with my spiritual gift.

Q3. What is my responsibility to receive from other Christians?

A3. My responsibility to receive from other Christians is to allow them to *love* me and *serve* me with their gift.

Chapter 6

Q1. What does the Bible teach about the role of time in spiritual growth?

A1. The Bible teaches that spiritual growth requires *time,* just as physical growth does.

Q2. What does the Bible teach about the role of trials in spiritual growth?

A2. The Bible teaches that trials are used by God to make us spiritually insightful and *strong.*

Q3. What examples does the Bible give us of the role of time and trials?

A3. The Bible gives us many examples of spiritual leaders whose trials eventually produced spiritual *maturity.*

Chapter 7

Q1. What decision does faith demand from me?

A1. Faith demands total *commitment* to God.

Q2. What motivation does faith give me?

A2. Faith motivates the Christian to be totally *obedient.*

Q3. What strength does faith give me?

A3. Faith gives me the strength to *persevere* in the face of trials.

Chapter 8

Q1. What is an entrenched sin?

A1. Entrenched sin is *chronic* sin that a Christian has a difficult time getting consistent victory over.

Q2. How does sin get entrenched?

A2. Sin usually gets entrenched when we indulge small sins which *gradually* become bigger ones.

Q3. Why is entrenched sin so bad?

A3. Entrenched sin can *debilitate* the Christian and even destroy the one who does not escape.

Q4. How can the Christian gain victory over entrenched sin?

A4. The Christian can gain victory over entrenched sin by *repenting* and *receiving* the grace of God.

Chapter 9

Q1. Why must I minister to others?

A1. The commands of Christ, the teaching of Scripture, and the needs around us demand that we *accept* the challenge of ministering to others.

Q2. How does ministry stimulate spiritual growth?

A2. Outreach stimulates spiritual growth by *stretching* the Christian beyond his present level and bringing about learning, maturation, and fulfillment.

Q3. For what ministries is the Christian responsible?

A3. The Christian is *responsible* for evangelism, edification, and humanitarianism.

Q4. How do we remain motivated for the sacrifice of ministry?

A4. We remain motivated for the sacrifice of outreach by remembering it is an *obligation* because of what Christ and others have done for us.

Chapter 10

Q1. What is the role of meditation in spiritual growth?

A1. Meditation allows the Holy Spirit to renew the mind and provide deep *illumination* of spiritual truth.

Q2. What is the role of prayer in spiritual growth?

A2. Prayer is *conversation* with God which allows for requests to be made, communion to be experienced, and reconciliation to the will of God to be realized.

Q3. What is the role of fasting in spiritual growth?

A3. Fasting allows a high level of concentration and physical deprivation which heightens *spiritual* sensitivity.

Chapter 11

Q1. What is the role of simplicity in spiritual growth?

A1. Simplicity is an inward reality that manifests itself in a simplified outward *lifestyle* that frees one from many worldly bondages.

Q2. What is the role of solitude in spiritual growth?

A2. Solitude allows the Christian to free himself from the *distraction* of the world long enough to make wise, God-centered decisions and develop wise, God-centered perspectives.

Q3. What is the role of submission in spiritual growth?

A3. Submission generates a trust in the *sovereignty* of God that frees the Christian from fear and resentment over the way others treat us, and helps build a love for others.

Chapter 12

Q1. What is the role of confession in spiritual growth?

A1. Repentance and confession *restore* moral integrity and authority.

Q2. What is the role of worship in spiritual growth?

A2. Worship is a responsibility of the Christian which, if taken seriously, will be *deepened* in his relationship with God.

Q3. What is the role of generosity in spiritual growth?

A3. Generosity requires and encourages a *detachment* from the things of this world, and demonstrates living for the next world.

About the Author

Dr. Max Anders is a pastor at heart who applies the truths of God's Word to people's everyday lives. An original team member with Walk Thru the Bible Ministries and pastor of a mega-church for a number of years before beginning his speaking and writing ministry, Max has traveled extensively, speaking to thousands across the country.

His books include *30 Days to Understanding the Bible, 30 Days to Understanding How to Live a Christian Life, 30 Days to Understanding What Christians Believe,* as well as the other titles in this series. He holds a Master of Theology degree from Dallas Theological Seminary and a doctorate from Western Seminary in Portland, Oregon.

* * *

If you are interested in having Max Anders speak at your conference, church, or special event, please call interAct Speaker's Bureau at 1-800-370-9932.